Hardin

ANGLO-SAXON INFLUENCE
ON
WESTERN CHRISTENDOM
600–800

SPECULUM HISTORIALE
GENERAL EDITOR: DENIS SINOR

LATINS IN THE LEVANT
(1204-1566) by W. Miller

BENEDICTINE MONACHISM
by Dom Cuthbert Butler, with a Foreword by Dom David Knowles

ILLUSTRATIONS OF THE HISTORY OF MEDIEVAL THOUGHT AND LEARNING
by R. L. Poole, Second Edition, revised

THE GOTHIC HISTORY OF JORDANES
in English Version with an Introduction and Commentary by C. C. Mierow

ARTHUR OF BRITAIN
by E. K. Chambers, with a supplementary bibliography

ANGLO-SAXON INFLUENCE
ON
WESTERN CHRISTENDOM
600–800

By
S. J. CRAWFORD

CAMBRIDGE: SPECULUM HISTORIALE
NEW YORK: BARNES & NOBLE, INC

Originally published by the Oxford University Press in 1933
Reprinted, by permission, in 1966
for

SPECULUM HISTORIALE
42 Lyndewode Road, Cambridge

PRINTED IN GREAT BRITAIN
BY LOWE AND BRYDONE (PRINTERS) LTD, LONDON

PREFACE

THE sudden death of Dr. S. J. Crawford in December 1931 removed from among us the greatest living authority on a critical period of Anglo-Saxon and West European history. The enormous part played by Anglo-Saxon civilization in supporting and building up the Western world is only slowly coming to be realized. Upon the whole of the Anglo-Saxon period, but above all upon the age of St. Boniface, the knowledge of Dr. Crawford was unrivalled, and these lectures, delivered under the auspices of the University of London at University College in April and May 1931, will be invaluable to all who wish to understand either the literature or the history of the 'Dark Ages'. Those who had the advantage of hearing the lectures delivered will agree that they embody solid scholarship which will render them indispensable for many years to come.

R. W. CHAMBERS.

CONTENTS

Preface by R. W. CHAMBERS v

I. THE POSITION OF THE PAPACY IN THE SIXTH AND SEVENTH CENTURIES 1

II. THE ANGLO-SAXONS ON THE CONTINENT IN THE LATER SEVENTH AND EIGHTH CENTURIES 32

III. ANGLO-SAXON ENGLAND AND THE TRANSMISSION OF ANCIENT CULTURE . . 72

I

THE POSITION OF THE PAPACY IN THE SIXTH AND SEVENTH CENTURIES

Introduction.

WHILE we have many books and articles in English dealing with the conversion of the Anglo-Saxons from the standpoint of English history, we have not hitherto (so far as I know) had any study of the subject from the Roman point of view. Yet there can be no doubt that Anglo-Saxon studies gain incalculably in significance, as well as in vital human interest, when they are viewed against their European background. Accordingly in this short course of lectures my object is to show that, far from being a sphere of knowledge which may be safely relegated to professional antiquaries, Anglo-Saxon history and literature are an integral and indispensable element in literary and historical studies, because the subsequent development of Europe depended largely on decisions made in Anglo-Saxon England between A.D. 600 and 800.

The Position of the Roman See at the Accession of St. Gregory. The value and importance of the work accomplished by Gregory the Great cannot be understood without some reference to the position of the Papacy at his accession. At first sight it might appear that the reign of the Emperor Justinian (A.D. 527–65), which re-established Catholicism as the official creed of the

Empire, and won back Italy, Africa, and part of Spain from the Arian Ostrogoths, Vandals, and Visigoths, must have been an unmixed gain to the See of Rome, and have confirmed its supremacy. But in truth this was far from being the case. Even in the sixth century under so Catholic a sovereign as Justinian there was a very real danger that the oecumenical claims of the See of St. Peter might be overlooked between an eastern emperor, who regarded himself as head not only of the State but also of the Church, and the Teutonic national Churches in which bishops were increasingly looked upon as state officials and appointed with little or no reference to the wishes of the Pope or the interests of the Church. Indeed under popes like Agapetus and the unfortunate Vigilius closer union between the Papacy and the Emperor had restricted rather than extended the authority of the See of Rome. Whatever external unity had been attained by the recovery of Africa from the Vandals and Andalusia from the Visigoths was being destroyed by religious strife, which weakened even the spiritual supremacy of the popes. Moreover, the difficulties of the Papacy were further complicated by the invasion of Italy by the Lombards, a horde of half-Arian, half-heathen Teutons, who poured down into Italy in 568 to take possession of the seats vacated by the Ostrogoths. In one respect the Lombards formed the greatest danger of all, since their Arianism and their proximity to Rome were a constant threat to the very existence of the Papacy. A minor difficulty was the fact that Aquileia, the seat of the metropolitan of Istria, with jurisdiction in northern

THE POSITION OF THE PAPACY

Italy, was in a state of schism with Rome. But what of the other western provinces of the Empire which had once acknowledged the spiritual supremacy of the See of St. Peter?

Spain. Since the time of Euric (*c.* 478), all Spain, except the north-western corner, where the Catholic Suevi still held out, had been ruled by the Arian Visigoths. Arianism had been a redoubtable foe of Catholicism in the fifth century, and its influence was still far from negligible. But its power in the West had been broken by the overthrow of the Ostrogoths and the conversion of Clovis to Catholicism in 496, with the consequent collapse of the great Arian league founded by Theodoric the Great upon family alliances between the royal houses of the Ostrogoths, Visigoths, and Burgundians. By the third quarter of the sixth century, Spanish Arianism was hemmed in by a ring of Catholic states, and we find Athanagild marrying his daughters Brunhildis and Galswintha to the Catholic Merovingians Sigibert and Chilperic. Worse, however, than the foes without were the foes within. Spain was rent by dissension and hatred between Goths and Romans, and the kingship was so weakened by the extinction of the old royal house, which was followed by the rise and fall of one military adventurer after another, that the country became a theatre of incessant religious strife and civil war. The accession of Leovigild seemed for a time to suggest that Arianism might be established on a strong footing, but his son Reccared saw that the salvation of his kingdom lay in the adoption of Catholicism, which was proclaimed in 589 as the national creed of Spain. With the extinction of the house of Leovigild, Spain, in spite of the efforts of one or two able sovereigns, fell back into a state of anarchy, in which the Spanish Church reached a degree of degradation lower than that of the nobility, and the kingdom of the Visigoths fell an easy prey to the Saracens in the year 711. In the last chapter I shall have occasion to note that amid all its troubles the Spanish Church did not lack learning, and to emphasize the debt of medieval culture to Isidore of Seville.

But whether Arian or Catholic, the Spanish Church was governed and disciplined without reference to the Papacy, and was to all intents and purposes at this period a national Church.

Gaul. Outside Italy the centre of gravity of Catholicism in the West lay in Gaul. The Church of Gaul had been in the past a very arsenal of the Faith, rivalling even the Church of Africa in the number and importance of its saints, doctors, and scholars. In the fourth and fifth centuries it had reckoned among its alumni St. Hilary of Poitiers, Paulinus of Nola, Sulpicius Severus, Marius Victor, Hilary of Arles, Prosper of Aquitaine, Vincent of Lerins, Sidonius Apollinaris, Avitus of Vienne, Ennodius, Caesarius of Arles, and others, whose names are a sufficient index of the intimate relations between the Church of Gaul and the rest of the Western Church—the Papacy in particular.

But in spite of the conversion of the Franks to the Catholic Faith, and in spite of the undoubted growth of both secular and monastic clergy in prestige and influence among the Franks, the sixth and particularly the second half of the seventh centuries were on the whole an era in which ecclesiastical discipline was being relaxed and the sanctions of morality weakened. It would no doubt be easy to paint the spiritual condition of the Frankish Church under the Merovings in too gloomy colours, and to lay too great stress on the implications in the narrative of Gregory of Tours or on the acts of church councils. The acts of councils show that there were many bishops in the sixth century anxious to enforce ecclesiastical discipline, and the *Lives of the Saints*—making every allowance for the peculiar procedure of the hagiographer—show us that all over Gaul there were men and women of holy and even saintly character striving to practise Christian perfection as they understood it. Among the bishops were men like Caesarius of Arles, Nicetus of Lyons, Avitus Paternus of Avranches and others of holy exemplary life, who deserved the love and veneration of their flocks for the protection which they afforded to the oppressed and their unbounded liberality to the poor.

Yet when every allowance is made, the condition of the Frankish Church in the sixth and seventh centuries was not reassuring. The accession of the Merovings to Catholicism had not been an unmixed blessing for the Church in Gaul. It had placed the Church under the shadow of the Crown. Catholics though they were, the Merovings did not differ very much from their Arian fellow sovereigns in their treatment of the Church.

They regarded it as a national rather than as an international organism. While most of them did lip-service to the papal supremacy, in actual practice they recognized no authority in the kingdom as superior to their own will, and their claim appears to have been admitted by the bishops. For a time the metropolitan of Arles had legatine authority in Gaul, but even the authority of so great a pope as Gregory I was purely moral. Theudebert consulted him on a question of marriage law, but this is about the only example of any recognition of the pope's right to interfere in the internal affairs of the Frankish kingdoms. It is curious that the pope should be mentioned only seven times by Gregory of Tours, and not even once by so devout a catholic as Venantius Fortunatus. The affairs of the Frankish Church were discussed and settled in national councils where the king's influence was paramount. It could hardly have been otherwise, since Clovis and his successors had riveted their authority upon the clergy by refusing to allow a layman to be ordained without the royal licence, by the ever-increasing pressure which they exercised upon the election of bishops, and by even controlling the proceedings at the church councils. No doubt the traditional Teutonic loyalty to the kingship also tended to promote the freer exercise of the royal will in ecclesiastical affairs in proportion as the number of Franks in ecclesiastical orders increased.

It might perhaps have been expected that monasticism, which was a marked feature of the Church in Gaul from the time of St. Martin of Tours and did much to renovate and revitalize Christianity in Gaul in the days of the Merovings, would have proved an antidote to the growing secularization of the Church. But Gallic monasticism in the sixth century was restricted in its influence by the absence of a uniform monastic rule (some monasteries being subject to older rules like those of St. Basil or St. Cassian, and others having adopted newer rules such as that of Caesarius of Arles and later on that of St. Columbanus or Benedict of Nursia), and by the subjection of the monasteries to the episcopal authority, which rendered it difficult for them to offer any serious opposition whenever the bishop happened to be unworthy of his office.

At all events during the period extending from about 639 to 741, which witnessed the feudalization of the Frankish state, the fall of the Merovingian dynasty, and the rise to power of the new royal house of the Arnulfings, the process of secularization went on steadily. The wealth of the Church, which had grown enormously, became increasingly the object of the avaricious designs of both kings and nobles. Nor can it be said that the Arnulfings, in spite of their ecclesiastical origins, were any more scrupulous in their treatment of the Church than the Merovings. Charles Martel removed recalcitrant bishops, and appointed his own nominees to vacant sees. A bishopric or rich abbey became the usual reward of political services. Simony was everywhere rife, and men devoid of spiritual vocation and without the requisite literary qualifications were to be found occupying high positions in the Church. The organization of the Church was breaking down and contending authorities were frequently found within the same diocese. The office of metropolitan became obsolete, and for eighty years before the coming of St. Boniface the national councils had ceased to function. Secular-minded bishops had little to distinguish them from lay nobles, and not infrequently spent their time in war or hunting. Many clerics abandoned their orders, and found a ready refuge from the penalties of their crimes in the protection of some neighbouring noble. Even apostate monks were not uncommon. As early as the time of St. Columbanus, monastic discipline had become lax in so famous a house as Lerins. Learning, too, except of the most elementary kind, had fallen into decay, and the Church of Gaul had made no contribution of any importance to either secular or sacred letters since the death of Gregory of Tours. A symptom of the prevailing anarchy was the fact that paganism was lifting up its head and idolatrous practices mingling with the rites of the Church in some parts of Gaul.

The Celtic Churches. In the course of our survey of the condition of the Church in the West, we have now to deal with the Celtic Church.

At the time of the fall of the Roman Empire in the West there was an organized Christian Church in Britain in full communion with the Catholic Church in the West. The first date in the history of the British Church is 314, when three British bishops were present at the council of Arles. Sulpicius Severus tells us that three British bishops of questionable orthodoxy took part in the council of Rimini in 359. But in 363 we have the high authority of St. Athanasius for the orthodoxy of the British Church. In the first quarter of the fifth century, St. Ninian, who was of British birth though educated at Rome, carried the faith to the heathen of Galloway, and built a stone church at Whitern, which he dedicated to St. Martin of Tours. Somewhere about the same time the British Church produced a man of outstanding ability in the arch heretic Pelagius. Pelagianism seems to have had considerable attraction for the Celtic Church, and it was only eradicated with the help of St. Germanus of Auxerre, St. Lupus of Troyes, and St. Severus of Trier. The interposition of the Church of Gaul shows how intimate was the relationship between the two Churches, and further proof of the close connexion between Gaul and Britain may be found in the widespread influence of St. Martin of Tours upon the British Church, which embodied his ideals in its monastic system. We have already seen that St. Ninian's new church at Whitern was dedicated to St. Martin, as was also the old church at Canterbury handed over to St. Augustine by King Ethelbert.

The Barbarian Invasions broke the continued development of the British Church as an integral portion of the Western Church, though it never ceased to be Catholic in doctrine, and to acknowledge the spiritual supremacy of the successors of St. Peter, even if it may have failed to keep pace with the subsequent development of papal claims. It may, we think, be justly said that the later differences between the Roman and Celtic Churches were for the most part constitutional rather than doctrinal; they related to the proper method of reckoning the date of Easter, the form of the tonsure, the method of administering baptism, and the question whether it was necessary to have more than one bishop at an episcopal ordination. Their variations from the Roman and continental practice were due almost entirely to the insular development of the British Churches after the middle of the fifth century.

Trifling as most of these differences may seem to us, it would be foolish to under-estimate their effect in the sixth and seventh centuries. They were serious enough to separate the Breton Church from the rest of the Frankish Church in spite of all the efforts made by the Archbishop of Tours to enforce his authority, while in England we find Theodore of Tarsus ordaining in one of his canons that those who are doubtful regarding the validity of their baptism by Scottish or British dissenters may be rebaptized—a concession which is contrary to Catholic practice and doctrine. Aldhelm in his Letter to Gerontius regards the British Christians as 'heretics and schismatics', and sums up in the significant words: 'Utterly in vain is it for those who reject the doctrine and the rule of St. Peter to boast of their Catholicism.'

In our judgement it was in the best interests of the Christian Faith and certainly in the best interests of civilization in the Dark Ages, that the states of western Europe should be linked together in common membership of a universal Church and that an all-pervading centralized authority should be imposed upon the ecclesiastical development of the young Christian Churches of the West. That this centralization of authority entailed limitation upon human freedom cannot be denied; but freedom in the Dark Ages often spelt spiritual and national anarchy. There can be no true freedom apart from discipline, and this was just the element in which the Celts were weak.

The characteristics of the British Church were to be found in the Irish Church, but in an enhanced degree. The origins of Christianity in Ireland are obscure: all that is certain is that there were Christians in Ireland before Palladius and St. Patrick, who are regarded by Zimmer on inadequate grounds as one and the same person. But whether we ascribe the origin of Irish Christianity to the old British Church, or to the Church of Gaul, or to Pope Celestine, the results of the mission were so fruitful that by the sixth century Irish Christianity surpassed that of every other land in western Europe, not only in intensity and sanctity, but also in passionate devotion to learning and missionary enthusiasm.

In contrast with Roman Christianity, the organization of the Celtic Church was tribal and monastic. Bishops and priests were attached to the tribe and the monastery, and the limits of episcopal jurisdiction were ill defined. In all matters of discipline the abbot (who was frequently, but not necessarily, a bishop) was supreme, and bishops were under his jurisdiction.

In the sixth and seventh centuries Ireland was covered with monasteries in which the disciplinary practices of the monks of the Thebaid and their imitators at Lerins and other monasteries of southern Gaul in the days of St. Martin had been combined with the application of the arts of the trivium and quadrivium, handed down from the Graeco-Roman World, to the study of the Scriptures. Such a union of asceticism and learning existed nowhere else at this date.

But the most striking feature of Irish Christianity was its tendency to expansion. Irish Christianity exhibited something of the missionary passion of the apostolic age, and hundreds, even thousands, of the Irish were embracing voluntary exile for the sake of Christ and the Gospel when the rest of Christendom was either marking time, or even yielding ground before the advance of Mohammedanism. No doubt the restless temper of the Celt and his love for ascetic practice played their part in this movement; but the history of Iona and the career of St. Columbanus of Luxeuil show the inadequacy of a purely psychological explanation of the Celtic missions, and prove that the *peregrini*, as they were called, were *peregrini* not for their own sake, but, to use one of their favourite terms, *peregrini pro Christo*.

These apostolic migrations of the Celts are associated mainly with two great names, Columba and Columbanus, though they had many predecessors. We all know the story of St. Columba, how he left Ireland in 563-5, *praedicaturus uerbum Dei*, to use the words of Bede, and established the great missionary settlement of Iona, with many subordinate monasteries from which the Faith spread over Pictish Scotland, and southward to England. For the details of the life of St. Columba it is enough to refer to the famous life by his disciple Adamnan, noting that Rome neither initiated nor controlled the missions from Iona, and that St. Columba died on 9 June 597, seven days before Ethelbert of Kent was baptized by St. Augustine.

The other outstanding name in the history of the Celtic Mission Church is that of St. Columbanus. Born in Leinster about the year 543, he was educated, like his illustrious comrade St. Gall, at the monastery of Bangor in northern Ireland. Columbanus was already a man past his middle age when he left Ireland 'to spread the gospel among foreign peoples'. He landed in Gaul, where, as we learn from his biographer Jonas, he found indeed the Christian Faith, but 'it possessed neither the medicine of penance nor the love of ascetic discipline'. Columbanus reached Burgundy in the year of Gregory the Great's election to the Papacy. In Burgundy he founded in succession the monasteries of Anegray, Luxeuil, and Fontaines, all of which were under the jurisdiction of Columbanus and governed by his rule, which was based on Irish principles and imposed rigorous spiritual discipline, including the practice of confession, penance, and self-mortification. The zeal and saintliness of Columbanus and his companions excited the reverence and admiration of the people of Burgundy, and in spite of or rather because of their severe discipline the first foundations were soon filled to overflowing with the youth of Burgundy. Columbanus himself became a father-confessor to high and low, monks and laymen. The rule of St. Columbanus spread with great rapidity, and new monasteries arose all over the Frankish dominions in which the stricter discipline was adopted. In certain monasteries the rule of St. Columbanus was combined with other rules; and mixed monasteries, of the same type as that of St. Hild at Whitby, were also established.

The combination of asceticism and moral perfection which we find in the rule of St. Columbanus was not in itself a novelty in the Gallic Church, nor was the enforcement of obedience even unto death. But what did characterize the rule of St. Columbanus and set it apart from its rivals was the rigorous energy with which it was enforced and practised. The closest analogy to Columbanus that we can think of is John the Baptist in his attitude to the religion of the Jewish Church.

That a man of the prophetic temper of Columbanus would be able to pursue his course unhindered was not to be expected. Even before the death of Gregory the Great he had come into conflict both with the king and with the diocesan bishops of Gaul. The truth is that for a time at least the mission of St. Columbanus in Gaul was a church within a church. Irish Christianity with its monastic organization, its archaic Easter reckoning, its peculiar penitential system, and its distinct methods of baptism and of consecration of bishops was transplanted to Gaul, and little or no attempt appears to have been made by Columbanus to conciliate the authorities of the Frankish Church or the Papacy by assimilating his practices to those in operation around him. There is no evidence, for example, that he obtained the leave of the bishops, as required by the constitution of the Frankish Church, before establishing a monastery in their dioceses. He disregarded the authority of the diocesan by calling in an Irish bishop to consecrate an altar in his new church at Luxeuil. Not even the authority of the Pope himself could shake the determination of Columbanus to follow the Celtic practice in reckoning the date of the Easter festival, which was a perennial source of conflict between the Irish and the diocesan bishops.

The reports received at Rome from Candidus, the administrator of the papal estates in Gaul, regarding the attitude of the Celts to ecclesiastical authority, cannot have been of a reassuring character.

Meantime the moral earnestness of Columbanus had brought upon him the enmity of Theuderich, the young king of Burgundy, and, what was more serious, the hostility of his grandmother Brunhildis. Whatever may have been the merits of this famous lady (and among them may be reckoned the fact that she was a correspondent of Gregory the Great), she was no friend to Columbanus. Jonas, the biographer of Columbanus, expressly charges her with encouraging the debauchery of her grandson in order to secure her own authority.

On one occasion, he tells us, when Columbanus visited the court, Brunhildis presented the illegitimate sons of Theuderich to Columbanus and asked him to bless them. The saint abruptly refused, prophesying that these boys would never inherit the throne because they were bastards. Jonas also informs us that Columbanus lashed the vices of Theuderich in his letters to him, and threatened him with excommunication if he did not change his ways.

Brunhildis was not the woman to bear this with patience, and she determined to get rid of Columbanus; she had the bishops as well as the king on her side. The result was that Columbanus was banished from Burgundy in A.D. 610. After lengthy wanderings through Neustria and Austrasia, he betook himself to Switzerland, and fixed his dwelling near Lake Zurich. But his fiery zeal which led him to destroy with his own hands their temples and idols brought upon him the fury of the heathen, and once more he was forced to flee, this time to Bregenz. Here he worked for three years unmolested, until the conquest of Bregenz by Theuderich compelled him to escape across the Alps into Lombardy, leaving his monastery to the care of St. Gall, under whose name it afterwards became famous. In Lombardy Columbanus was received with honour by King Agilulf and his queen, Theodelinda, who presented him with a district on the Trebbia, between Genoa and Milan, where he established the great monastery of Bobbio. There he died in the year 615.

Yet, before his death, Columbanus had been able to

perform one further service to the Catholic Church by bringing the weight of Irish Catholic tradition and learning to the support of Agilulf and Theodelinda in their struggle with the Arianism of their Lombard subjects. The struggle, complicated as it was by the schism in the Church at Aquileia, was long continued, and only finally decided in favour of Catholicism in 680. The Papacy must share the credit for the victory with Theodelinda, and not less with Columbanus and his successors at Bobbio. It would not be easy to deal adequately with the extent to which the Celtic Church affected the Continent. The subject has been treated at length by scholars such as Zimmern, Hauck, Gougaud, and very recently by Kenney. It may suffice here to say that before the eighth century there were at least fifty important centres where Irish influence was dominant, ranging from Brittany in the north-west and Angoulême to Disibodenberg, Würzburg, and Salzburg in the east, and from the English Channel and the coast of Belgium through St. Gall to Bobbio in the south. A glance at a map will show how the influence of the Celts pervaded north-western Europe at this period, and suggest how dangerous a rival Celtic Christianity might have proved to Rome had it been allowed to remain outside the centralized authority of the Papacy.

Our long survey is ended. In spite of its length it is very inadequate, but it is to be hoped that enough has been said to suggest the actual weakness of papal authority in the sixth and seventh centuries, not only in Italy but throughout the West, and how strong were the forces which threatened the disruption of Catholic unity in spite of the general recognition of the claims of Rome to the primacy.

The position was saved by the accession of Gregory the Great, and the adhesion of the Anglo-Saxons to Roman Christianity.

Gregory the Great. Taking him for all in all, St. Gregory was the greatest of the popes, whether we judge him by his qualities as a man, or as a statesman, or by his saintly character. As a scholar he had decided limitations: the bent of his mind was practical rather than metaphysical—but, even so, it is doubtful whether Augustine himself had a more profound influence as a doctor of the Church.

On his accession to the Papacy in A.D. 590, Gregory found the moral and spiritual supremacy of the Roman See severely weakened by a succession of popes who had been wanting in the ability and personality requisite to cope with the unparalleled difficulties and problems presented by the Barbarian Invasions and the consequent downfall of the Roman Empire in the West. In place of a united Church in a united Empire, disintegration and disruption were apparent on every side,[1] and the successor of St. Leo saw himself in danger of becoming the puppet of a barbarian and heretical king or, at best, the instrument of the statecraft of an eastern emperor

[1] On the condition of Italy, see A. W. Clapham, *English Romanesque Architecture before the Conquest*, p. 16 (Oxford 1930).

almost equally antagonistic to the independence of the Papacy and the highest interests of the Catholic Faith.

It would, we believe, be a grievous error to imagine that the modern distinction between the extension of the authority and discipline of the Roman Church and the extension of the Christian Faith had any existence in the mind of St. Gregory. For him they were one and the same thing. When St. Gregory aimed at re-establishing the lost or weakened supremacy of the Papacy over the West, we cannot doubt that he was actuated solely by consideration for the supreme good of the Faith. It is important to be clear in our minds about this point, for, of the manifold aspects of the work of Gregory the Great, it is with his missionary activities that we are now chiefly concerned.

Judged from the standpoint of his own times, Gregory's policy did not imply any extension of claims or any expansion of the jurisdiction of the Church. So far as we can judge, he, unlike the Celts, made no attempt to invade on behalf of the Church any province beyond the borders of the old Roman Empire. Had his primary object been the winning of new peoples for the Faith, he could have found, just beyond the Alps, heathen much easier of access than the distant Anglo-Saxons. But Britain was a lost province not only of the Roman Empire but of the Roman Church. This, however, may not have been Gregory's only reason for the choice of Britain as a Roman mission centre. We are not referring now to the well-known story of the Anglo-

Saxon boys in the slave-market at Rome—which may be authentic: it was current in the early eighth century, and there seems to be no good reason for rejecting it. What we have in mind is the more important question how far the imperative necessity of co-ordinating the activities of the energetic Celtic Church with the policy of the See of Rome, and of utilizing the Celtic capacity for missionary propaganda and intense personal devotion in the service of the Church as a whole, was a determining factor in the selection of Britain. We have no definite evidence that it was, though it may well have been so.

In the first place Gregory's scheme of bishoprics for the Anglo-Saxon Church provided for the reorganization of the British monastic churches under the primacy of Augustine. Moreover, the Celtic missions associated with the names of Columba and Columbanus both precede the Roman mission to Britain. The life of Columba was closing when Augustine landed in England and Columbanus had been working in Gaul for five years in 595, when we first hear of the contemplated mission to the Anglo-Saxons. Gregory had an agent in Candidus, who may have come into contact with Columbanus in 595–6, and at any rate must have had much to report regarding the popularity and progress of the Celts in Burgundy. Gregory was too great a statesman to be oblivious to the dangers of a Church, however notable for orthodoxy, sanctity, and learning, which refused to submit to the authority of the diocesans, and, at any rate in the person of its leader, showed itself ready on occasion to maintain and justify its irregular practices even against the Pope himself. But, whether this was first realized by Gregory or by his successors, the complete Romanization of the Celtic Churches of Britain afforded the best guarantee against the risks of schism whether on the Continent or in the British Isles. The victory of Rome was not easily won, even in England, where the struggle lasted some seventy years.

The Mission of St. Augustine. The story of the mission of St. Augustine is so familiar that the details need not detain us. As with Clothilde and Clovis, Theodelinda and Agilulf, Ethelburga and Edwin, and Eanflaed and Oswy, the Catholicism of the wife became the medium of Roman influence upon her husband. Bertha secured a favourable reception for the missionaries. As Bede tells us:

'It was not the first time that he [Ethelbert of Kent] had heard of the Christian religion: because, in fact, he had a Christian wife of the royal family of the Franks, who had been given to him by her parents on the understanding that she should be allowed to maintain, without interference, the system of her faith and religion, as well as a bishop named Liudhard, whom they had given as a helper of her faith.'[1]

It may have been through Liudhard that Gregory had heard that the English were well disposed to the Faith,[2] though the apparent apathy of Liudhard is typical of

[1] *H.E.* i. 25. [2] *Reg.* vi. 57.

the absence of missionary enthusiasm which prevailed in the Frankish Church. He is a striking contrast to Paulinus, who was similarly situated. In passing, it may be noted as curious that Ethelbert, who was married to a Christian wife and allowed her to practise her religion, should (according to Bede) have been so afraid that Augustine and his companions would practise witchcraft upon him that he received them in the open air and refused to allow them to approach his house. However this may have been, the immediate success of the missionaries was very great. As Bede says: 'To make a long story short, a good number believed and were baptized, wondering at their simple and innocent lives and at the charm of the heavenly doctrines.' The baptism of the king soon followed, and, as was usual among the Teutons, his subjects voluntarily imitated his example and 'forsook the heathen system to attach themselves as believers to the unity of Christ's holy Church'. The missionaries were soon given a place of settlement suitable to their condition in Ethelbert's capital of Canterbury. Indeed, so great was St. Augustine's success, that Gregory, whose noble personality and sanity of judgement are reflected through the whole correspondence, felt bound to warn him to rejoice not because the devils were subject unto him in Christ's name, but to rejoice rather because his name was written in heaven.

The conversion of Kent led Gregory to feel that the time was now ripe for a complete reorganization of the Church in Britain under the direction of Augustine,

THE POSITION OF THE PAPACY

who had been consecrated archbishop of the English by Vergilius of Arles, on instructions from Rome. The scheme outlined by Gregory would seem to have been suggested by the organization of the Romano-British Church in the days before the Anglo-Saxon conquest. It anticipated the conversion of the remainder of Anglo-Saxon England, and provided for two metropolitans, each with twelve bishops subject to his jurisdiction: the See of the southern metropolitan was to be at London, and that of the northern metropolitan at York. The honour of the primacy was to be shared between the archbishops according to seniority, though in other respects there was to be equal division of authority. The apostasy of Essex prevented the primacy being removed from Canterbury to London. That Gregory intended the jurisdiction of Augustine to include not only the newly converted Anglo-Saxons, but also the Celtic Churches of Britain, and perhaps Iona, is clear from his response to the Seventh Question of Augustine, where he says:

'But as for all the bishops of Britain, we commit them to your care, that the unlearned may be taught, the weak strengthened by persuasion, and the perverse corrected by authority.'[1]

Meantime, Gregory had sent Augustine the pallium indicating that he was to be regarded as representing the Roman See, and also reinforcements. Among the newcomers were Justus, consecrated Bishop of Rochester

[1] *H.E.* i. 27.

in 604, Mellitus, appointed to London in the same year, and Paulinus, the future apostle of Northumbria. When Augustine and Gregory died in 604, it must have seemed that in south-eastern England Christianity was firmly established both in the laws of King Ethelbert and in the hearts of the people.

But, great as had been Augustine's success in Kent, he had had one great failure which was destined to complicate the relations between Roman and Celtic Christianity in England for many years to come.

Conference with the British Bishops. The importance attached by Augustine to the recognition of his authority by the British Church is evident from the fact that no sooner did success seem to be assured in Kent than he proceeded to take in hand the discipline of the British Church. With the support of Ethelbert, somewhere between 600–3 he held two conferences with the British bishops, at which the points at issue soon appeared. Augustine said to them:

'You act in many particulars contrary to our custom, or rather to the custom of the universal Church, and yet, if you will comply with me in these three points, viz., to keep Easter at the due time; to administer baptism . . . according to the custom of the holy Roman Apostolic Church; and jointly with us to preach the word of God to the English nation, we will readily tolerate all the other things you do, though contrary to our custom.'

The British Church emphatically rejected Augustine's authority; and as long as they retained their separate Easter they were treated by Rome as schismatical. Yet

THE POSITION OF THE PAPACY

the uncompromising attitude, not to say tactlessness, of Augustine was not the sole reason for the failure of the conferences. Augustine came to the British bishops as the metropolitan of their bitterest foes, and they could not but see in submission to his authority the loss of both ecclesiastical and national independence.

Heathen Reaction. The success of the Roman mission was largely due to the support of the kings; and the deaths of Ethelbert in 616, and of Sæbert, king of Essex, were followed by a heathen reaction. Eadbald, the son of Ethelbert, lived in incest with his stepmother, while the heathen sons of Sæbert drove Mellitus from his See of London. He fled to Kent, where he joined Laurentius, who had succeeded Augustine as archbishop, and Justin of Rochester. All three decided to abandon the thankless land. Justin and Mellitus fled to Gaul, and Laurentius was only prevented by divine interposition from following them. The infant Church seemed to be on the verge of destruction, when suddenly Eadbald decided to become a Christian, and the situation was saved. Justin and Mellitus returned after a year's absence in Gaul, but the Londoners refused to receive Mellitus, and persisted in their apostasy. The action of Justin and Mellitus suggests one reason why the Anglo-Saxon Church of the seventh century had no martyrs. The position was now partially retrieved, but the Roman missionaries could now no longer depend upon the assistance of the kings of Kent, for the political supremacy had passed from Kent to Northumbria, and the future of Christianity in England hung upon the decision of the Angles.

Christianity in Northumbria, &c. The Northumbrian kingdoms of Deira and Bernicia had been united in 593 under Ethelfrith, the grandson of Ida of Bernicia. Ethelfrith was a mighty warrior—'the strongest of kings', says Bede,[1] 'and the most greedy of glory, but for the fact that he lacked knowledge of the true faith'. At the battle of Degsa stan, perhaps Dawston in Liddesdale, he had broken the power of Aedan and the Christian Scots of Dalriada, and extended his kingdom to the north-west. By a series of victories culminating in a notable battle at Chester, he had driven a wedge between the Welsh of Wales and those of Strathclyde, much as Ceawlin of Wessex by his victory at Dyrham in 577 had cut off the Welsh north of the Bristol Channel from those of Cornwall and the south-west. These victories made Northumbria the most powerful kingdom in England.

As Kent was no longer the predominant power in England, it was unable to exert the same influence on behalf of the Roman Church. The failure of the conferences of Augustine with the British bishops had destroyed all hope of securing the co-operation of the Welsh Churches—now further weakened and antagonized by the victories of Northumbria. It therefore became more imperative than ever to press on with the mission to the Anglo-Saxons.

So long as Ethelfrith lived, there seemed to be no oppor-

[1] *H.E.* i. 34.

tunity for doing so, and, for wellnigh a generation after Augustine, Roman Christianity was confined to Kent. The position changed in 625, and again feminine influence became the instrument of Roman policy. Ethelfrith had been overthrown in 617 by Rædwald of East Anglia. Edwin had become king of Northumbria with the help of Rædwald, and had made himself overlord of all England except Kent, with which he allied himself by marrying Ethelberga, the daughter of Ethelbert. She was accompanied to Northumbria by Paulinus as her chaplain, and by James the Deacon. Through their influence King Edwin was baptized in the year 627, and the future seemed full of hope for the realization of the plans of Gregory the Great. Paulinus, who had baptized multitudes of the Northumbrians, became bishop of York, and Edwin co-operated with him zealously in advancing the Faith, which spread through Lindsey and East Anglia. A church was built at Lincoln by Paulinus, and Felix of Burgundy became bishop of Dunwich.

But a great disaster was impending. The conquests of Northumbria, and possibly also the zeal which Edwin showed in propagating the new faith, brought about a great coalition of his enemies. Cadwallon of Gwynedd united the Welsh in a national struggle against the hated invaders, and found a ready ally in the heathen Penda of Mercia. The result was the complete overthrow of Edwin at the battle of Hatfield in 633. Edwin and his son were slain, and Queen Ethelberga fled to Kent, accompanied by Paulinus. The battle of Hatfield was followed by the apostasy of the Northumbrians. James the Deacon was the only representative of the Roman Church left in Northumbria, where Christianity seemed to be extinct.

The supremacy of Northumbria, but not of the Roman Church, was restored by Oswald's victory at 'Denisesburn' in 634, where Cadwallon fell, and with him all the hopes of the Welsh regaining their power in the north and stemming the tide of Anglo-Saxon conquest.

In Oswald Christianity found a devoted champion, whose enthusiasm for religion was founded on personal conviction rather than on political motives. But Oswald's Christianity came from Iona and not from Rome, and it was to Iona, therefore, and not to Canterbury, that he sent for helpers to fill the places left vacant by the flight of Paulinus and the Roman missionaries. How the combined labours of Oswald and Aidan established Celtic Christianity on a firm basis in Northumbria is a well-known story. The monks of Iona took up the English mission with their characteristic fervour and enthusiasm. In a short time the monastic organization, ascetic discipline, and intense missionary propaganda were planted in Northumbria, under the direction of Aidan. The great monastery of Lindisfarne became a second Iona from which religion and learning radiated over England for a period of thirty years. The work begun by Oswald was continued under Oswy. One after another the strongholds of heathenism in the north and midlands fell before the Celtic missionaries. The Middle Angles and East Saxons became Christians in 653, followed by the Mercians in 655. The labours of the Burgundian Felix were supplemented by the work of the Irish Fursey about the same time. Wessex, on the other hand, owed its Christianity to Birinus and Pope Honorius—but not, be it observed, to Canterbury, which except perhaps in East Anglia had no practical influence on the general life and work of the Church. So great was the share of the Celtic Church in the conversion of England that Bishop Lightfoot has said: 'Augustine was the apostle of Kent, but Aidan was the apostle of England.'

Yet the ascendancy of the Celtic Church in England was destined to last only some thirty years. Had saintliness of life, missionary enthusiasm, and love for learning sufficed, their position would have been unassailable. But the Celtic Church was weakest where the Roman Church was strongest. The radical defect of Celtic Christianity was lack of organization. It is true that the Celtic monasteries and mission stations in England were subject to the abbot of Iona, but they possessed neither regular parochial nor diocesan organization. There may have been a growing consciousness that, in that age, unity of the Church was the first step to unity of the State. Yet, for some thirty years of the seventh century, there were really two independent Churches in Anglo-Saxon England, the Celtic in the north and midlands, and the Roman in the south.

But of more immediate importance was the fact that there had grown up in the shadow of the Celtic Church a younger school with a wider outlook, whose imagination had been captured by the ideals represented by the policy of the Papacy. The leader of this school of thought was Wilfrid of York, who may, we think, be regarded as the true heir of Gregory the Great in northern Europe. Men like Wilfrid of York longed to see the Church of England take its rightful place as one of the great provinces of the Western Church. For them (and who can say that they were wrong?) to be united with Rome was to be united with the main stream of Christian civilization, and to be safeguarded against all the dangers, whether national or religious, which in the Dark Ages threatened an isolated Church. Moreover, their reading of Christian Latin literature had filled them with something of that same veneration for the Eternal City which compelled its barbarian invaders to perform their work of destruction in the name of the emperors whom they were destroying.

Yet once again a woman's influence proved the way for a revolution of opinion in favour of the Roman party. Oswy's wife, Eanflæd, a princess of Kent, had remained loyal to her Roman Catholic upbringing. Around her were united various representatives of Roman influence in the north. Among these were James the Deacon, who had kept alive the tradition of Paulinus, a certain Scot called Ronan, who had learnt the Roman method of calculating Easter in Gaul or Italy,[1] Alchfrid the son of King Oswy, who had come under the influence of Wilfrid, and, above all, Wilfrid

[1] *H.E.* iii. 25.

THE POSITION OF THE PAPACY

himself. The Roman party in Northumbria were strengthened by the arrival of the Frank Agilbert, formerly bishop of the West Saxons, who had lost his See of Dorchester because he either could not or would not learn Anglo-Saxon. It is possible that Oswy had been already half-converted to the Roman view through his wife's influence. At all events he determined to call a conference, and, at the famous Synod of Whitby in 664, the Roman party, led by Agilbert, with Wilfrid as its spokesman, triumphed over Colman, Hild, and the supporters of the Celtic side. Colman and many of his friends left Northumbria, and the Roman party was left in possession of the field. At last there was to be uniformity throughout the English Church.

But the reorganization of the English Church on Roman lines was to be the work of Theodore of Tarsus, who arrived in England in 669, accompanied by Abbot Hadrian. The vision of Gregory the Great was largely realized by the Synod of Hertford some seventy years after his death. Roman, Celtic, and even Greek elements combined to make the last quarter of the seventh and the opening of the eighth century the golden age of the Anglo-Saxon Church, whose interposition on the Continent inaugurated a new era in the history of the Western Church in the Middle Ages.

II

THE ANGLO-SAXONS ON THE CONTINENT IN THE LATER SEVENTH AND EIGHTH CENTURIES

ANGLO-SAXON England has made two contributions of enduring value to the history of European civilization. The first is to be found in the missions of the Anglo-Saxon Church to Friesland and Germany in the late seventh and eighth centuries; the second is the life and work of Alfred the Great. The importance and significance of the latter has been universally recognized; but, in our own country at least, the contribution of the Anglo-Saxon Church to European culture has been largely ignored or forgotten except by scholars. Yet, if I am not mistaken, the European missions of the Anglo-Saxons were scarcely less momentous than the work of the great king for the future of medieval Europe.

A very remarkable feature of the missions is their national character. The more one studies the *Monumenta Moguntina, Alcuiniana, Carolina*, the *Acta Sanctorum*, Bede, and other sources for the history of the period, the more one is struck by the widespread interest taken in the new venture of the young Church. The missionaries were provided by every kingdom in the Heptarchy; and women were scarcely less numerous than men. Their work was followed with eager interest by friends and correspondents in every district of England, and even beyond it—from Thanet in the south-east to far-off Whitern in Galloway and Iona in the north, and from Exeter in the west to Dunwich and Lindisfarne by the North Sea. Kings and nobles (not all of unspotted life) vied with bishops, abbots, abbesses, nuns, and the lower ranks of the clergy and laity in the enthusiasm and admiration with which they regarded those who had voluntarily exiled themselves for Christ. The struggle between the missionaries of the infant Anglo-Saxon Church and their ancestral heathendom on the Continent struck the imagination of contemporaries, who saw in the enterprise of the warriors of the Cross a new heroic age in which the protagonists of the heroic lays were replaced by the saints, a Beowulf by a Willibrord and a Sigmund or a Sigurd by a Boniface—with a heavenly crown as the martyr's prize. To attempt to minimize, much more detract from, the value and merits of those who responded to the call to give up all things for Christ, is the last thing we should wish to do. At the same time it is impossible not to share the regret, suggested by the Venerable Bede, that the lure of the cloister and the call to exile for the sake of the heavenly crown should have deprived Anglo-Saxon England of the services of men and women whose character, courage, and personality would have been of incalculable value to the social and political life of the native kingdoms, and whose counsels and examples both in war and peace might have strengthened the fibre of the nation in the terrible crises of the Danish invasions, and averted the ruin which befell the moral and political life of eighth-century England. But such regrets are useless; and in any case our task is to show what the Continent gained rather than what England lost. In the eighth century, as in the eighteenth, perhaps the greatest work done by England is to be sought not at home but beyond the sea.

The immediate result of the Synod of Whitby was to end, in favour of the Roman party, the rivalry between the adherents of Rome and Iona within the English Church. To organize the administrative system of the Anglo-Saxon Church, to make the unity of the Church a model for the unity of the nation, and to establish at Canterbury a school in which the learning of the Empire, combined with the newer ideals of Church discipline and government, should be disseminated throughout England and far beyond it—all this was to be the work of Theodore of Tarsus during his tenure of the See of Canterbury from 669 to 690. The Roman party had won the day at Whitby; but it would be a great mistake to imagine that the Anglo-Saxon Church as organized by Theodore was a purely Roman creation. Far from it—the Anglo-Saxon Church of the later seventh and the eighth centuries was an English national Church, Roman in its organization, its discipline, and its orthodoxy, yet embodying ideals derived partly from the Celtic Church, partly from the Eastern Church, and most of all from the temper of the English people. The schools and scholars of Anglo-Saxon England owe little to the tradition of Gregory the Great and Augustine, but reflect Celtic and Greek ideals of sacred scholarship, while the life of Wilfrid is in itself a sufficient proof how far either Theodore and the English Church or the kings of Northumbria were from allowing the Papacy uncontrolled sway in the affairs of the national Church. But if the victory of Wilfrid and the Papacy was limited in England, the Papacy was destined to find its most devoted supporters in the Anglo-Saxon missionaries, who were almost without exception whole-heartedly in favour of the ideals for which Wilfrid stood. The foundations of the union between the Carolingians and the popes, on which the supremacy of the Catholic Church in the earlier Middle Ages rested, were laid by Willibrord, Boniface, and their companions and followers.

Enthusiasm for missionary work showed itself at a very early period in the history of the Anglo-Saxon Church. Wilfrid of York was born within eight years of the conversion of the Northumbrians by Paulinus, and Wilfrid's mission to Friesland in A.D. 678, which inaugurated the continental expansion of the Anglo-Saxon Church, took place eighty years after the landing of St. Augustine. This widespread impulse towards the mission-field was due to various causes. No doubt there was the obvious desire to fulfil the command 'to go into all the world and preach the gospel' and to bring salvation to those peoples who were sitting in darkness and in the shadow of death. But it should be noted that the first missionaries came from Northumbria; and it was just in Northumbria that the influence and example of the Celtic Church was strongest. Self-exile for the sake of Christ and the Gospel was perhaps the most marked characteristic of Irish Christianity, and it was passed on by the Irish to the Church of Northumbria. A second cause or impulse towards mission work among the continental Germans was the claims of kinship. Though some 200 years had passed since the Anglo-Saxon conquest of Britain, the invaders had never forgotten the ties which united them with the continental Teutons. The old traditions of their common life were kept alive in poetry. It is significant that all our extant heroic poetry in Anglo-Saxon deals with themes and events which belong to the heroic age on the Continent, and that not a single poem inspired by the conquest of Britain has been preserved, if indeed such ever existed. But apart from the work of poets, probably no race on the mainland was better known to the Anglo-Saxons than their kinsmen and neighbours the Frisians, who were the great seamen and traders of northern Europe in the seventh and eighth centuries.

Bede sums up these various motives in his account of Egbert:[1]

'At that time the venerable servant of Christ, and priest, Egbert, whom I cannot name but with the greatest respect, and who, as was said before[2] lived a stranger in Ireland to obtain hereafter a residence in heaven, proposed to himself to do good to many, by taking upon himself the apostolical work, and preaching the word of God to some of those nations that had not yet heard it: many of which nations

[1] *H.E.* v. 9. Cf. ibid. iii. 27, and see also *Monumenta Moguntina*, p. 304.
[2] *H.E.* iii. 27.

he knew were in Germany, from whom the Angles or Saxons, who now inhabit Britain are known to have derived their origin.... Such are the Frisians, the Rugini, the Danes, the old Saxons, and the Boructuarii.... To whom the aforesaid soldier of Christ designed to repair ... and to try whether he could deliver any of them from Satan, and bring them over to Christ.'[1]

To these various motives and impulses must be added the example and influence of a commanding personality. Wilfrid of York had already played an important role in ecclesiastical affairs by his intervention at the Synod of Whitby; and, so far as we can judge, he was the first among the Anglo-Saxons to grasp the supreme importance of securing the allegiance of the heathen Teutons for Christianity, and of extending the authority of the Papacy over central and north-eastern Europe. This may perhaps seem to be an overstatement, but I would point out that Wilfrid was the most zealous assertor in England of the rights of the Pope to spiritual pre-eminence, that he was at the same time an enthusiastic missionary, and that nearly all of the first generation of Anglo-Saxon missionaries came directly or indirectly under his influence, and, like him, were champions of the rights of Rome. Indeed, I do not think it is fanciful to find a parallel between the part played by the Anglo-Saxon missionaries in restoring and extending the waning supremacy of the Roman See in the eighth century with the part played by the Society

[1] Bede, v. 9.

of Jesus in the Counter-Reformation in the sixteenth century.

The history of Anglo-Saxon missions begins with the visit paid to Friesland in 678 by Wilfrid of York, who was on his way to Rome to lay his case against Egfrid of Northumbria and Archbishop Theodore before Pope Agathon. Bede implies that Wilfrid's visit to Friesland was accidental, and due to the fact that he was blown out of his course. But Eddi Stephanus, who had the best reasons for knowing the facts, since he accompanied Wilfrid, gives quite a different version. According to Eddi, Wilfrid chose the Frisian route to outwit his enemies, and in particular to avoid Ebroin the all-powerful mayor of the Palace of Neustria, whose hatred Wilfrid had incurred by helping Dagobert of Austrasia to gain his throne. Eddi does not mention contrary winds. His words are:

'Our holy bishop, with a west wind blowing gently according to his wish, and with the vessels heading eastward, came after a prosperous voyage to Friesland with all his companions. There he found great crowds of heathen, and was honourably received by King Aldgisl.'[1]

It does not look, therefore, as if it was a mere accident which brought Wilfrid to Friesland. Eddi further tells how Wilfrid preached the Faith to the heathen; and how (as similarly later on in Sussex) the effect of his preaching was confirmed by an unusually large catch of fish, so that nearly all the Frisian chiefs as well as

[1] Eddi Stephanus, *Life of Wilfrid*, xxvi.

thousands of the common people accepted baptism. Wilfrid spent the winter with King Aldgisl, who rejected with scorn the attempts of Ebroin to bribe him to betray Wilfrid, and finally in the spring of 679 sent him on his way to the court of his old friend Dagobert of Austrasia.

Thus we see that in 678 Friesland from the Sinkfal to the Weser and the Danish borders was a heathen land; though we know that as early as the reigns of Chlothar II and Dagobert I in the first half of the seventh century part of Friesland, including Utrecht, was under Frankish rule, and that some efforts had been made to christianize Frankish Friesland. These early missions are associated with the names of Amandus of Maestricht, Bavo, Kunibert of Köln, and Eligius of Noyon; but in the eighth century, as we learn from a letter of St. Boniface, the sole relic of the work of the Frankish Church among the Frisians was a ruined church at Utrecht over which the Bishop of Köln disputed jurisdiction with Boniface.

Wilfrid went on his way to Rome, and the story of his successful labours among the Frisians doubtless served to kindle the interest of the Roman See in the Frisian mission, and to prepare the way for the favourable reception accorded to Willibrord some eleven years later. But Wilfrid did not continue in person the work which he had begun in Friesland. When he was once more driven out of Northumbria, he found an outlet for his missionary enthusiasm in heathen Sussex (681–6) and had the glory of winning the last of the heathen kingdoms of England for the religion of the Cross. Wilfrid, however, did not forget Friesland, for we find him visiting Archbishop Willibrord there in 704 on his way to Rome, and Suidbert, the first bishop of the Frisians, was ordained by him. Ten years passed before Wilfrid found a successor in Friesland. This time the impulse came from Ireland. Egbert was a countryman of Wilfrid's. He was a Northumbrian of noble birth who, like so many Anglo-Saxons, had gone to Ireland for study and devotion. His beautiful character is among the finest in Bede, who cannot speak of him without admiration and reverence. In 689 Egbert was fired with the desire to preach the word of God among the heathen German tribes, but, as Bede tells us, when everything was ready, Egbert was prevented by a heavenly vision and a violent storm from pursuing his purpose:

'However Wictbert, one of his companions, being famous for his contempt of the world and for his knowledge, for he had lived for many years as a stranger in Ireland ... went abroad and arriving in Friesland (A.D. 689), preached the word of salvation for the space of two years successively to that nation and to its king Radbod; but reaped no fruit of all his great labour among his barbarous hearers. Then returning to his beloved place of exile, he gave himself up to the service of the Lord in his wonted silence.'[1]

Wictbert had found the situation in Friesland very different from what it had been when Wilfrid visited Aldgisl. Aldgisl was now dead, and his successor Radbod was engaged in a war of independence with the Franks

[1] Bede, *H.E.* v. 9.

THE ANGLO-SAXONS ON THE CONTINENT

led by Pippin of Heristal. Nationalism and heathenism had become synonymous with the Frisians, and to accept the religion of the Franks was to be false to Friesland. This change in the political situation is a sufficient explanation of the failure of Wictbert's mission.

Wictbert's place was filled almost at once by another Northumbrian, whose success has fairly earned for him the title of the Apostle of Friesland. St. Willibrord was born in 658 some time before his father Wigils (who is said by Alcuin[1] to have been of *Saxon* birth) forsook the world and retired to a cell at the mouth of the Humber. This very cell afterwards descended to Alcuin, who was a member of the same family as St. Willibrord. The young Willibrord was educated at Ripon under Wilfrid of York, then at the height of his influence. In A.D. 678, the year in which Wilfrid was banished from Northumbria, Willibrord, now twenty years old and an ordained monk, went to Egbert in Ireland. Though we have no definite statement to that effect, it seems most likely that Willibrord's retreat to Ireland was due to the banishment of his friend and master, St. Wilfrid; and it may well have been that Egbert's interest and enthusiasm for the propagation of the Faith among the kindred of the Anglo-Saxons beyond the seas was kindled by the arrival of Willibrord, whose master Wilfrid was able to send him such triumphant reports regarding the readiness of Aldgisl and his subjects to receive the Faith, and the protection which they had accorded him against the machinations of Ebroin and his enemies in

[1] *Vita Sancti Willibrordi*, ed. Jaffe, i. 1.

Neustria and Northumbria. The part played by Egbert in winning Iona to the Roman observance shows how closely he was in sympathy with St. Wilfrid and his policy.

However this may have been, Egbert refused to be discouraged by Wictbert's failure and, as Bede tells us, it was he who dispatched Willibrord to Friesland, accompanied, after the Irish fashion, by eleven companions, one of whom was the Anglo-Saxon Suidbert, who after having been consecrated regionary bishop of Friesland by Wilfrid, became the apostle of the heathen Bructeri, north of the Rhine and the Lippe, and died abbot of Kaiserwerth in 713. Somewhere about the same time falls the tragic and heroic story told by Bede of the two Hewalds, two missionary priests of English birth who had studied in Ireland and went to preach to the Old Saxons. The one brother, Black Hewald, was tortured and torn in pieces, the other, White Hewald, was dispatched with the sword. Their bodies were thrown into the Rhine. This is about all we know of the first Anglo-Saxon missionaries to the Saxons.

Willibrord and his companions landed at the mouth of the Rhine and set out at once for Utrecht. Conditions were not exactly favourable in Utrecht. Radbod had been defeated by Pippin and deprived of Friesland south of the Rhine, though he still held Utrecht. Defeat had left Radbod and the free Frisians resentful and antagonistic to Christianity. Willibrord decided that there was little hope of success for his work among the free Frisians; and that his best course was to turn to

Frankish Friesland, where with the assistance of Pippin he might be able to lay the foundations of a Frisian Church. The interests of the Church and the Frankish state appeared to be identical. Pippin of Heristal recognized in the christianization of the Frisians the guarantee of the Frankish dominion in Friesland. He therefore welcomed Willibrord and his companions, entered with alacrity into their plans, and aided them with all the means at his disposal. Thus was initiated that alliance between Church and State in the Carolingian Empire, which was to have such momentous results for both in the future, especially when united with a third factor, the Papacy. So far as we can judge it was the Anglo-Saxon Willibrord, the pupil of Wilfrid, and not the Frankish Mayor who demanded the consent of Rome to the Frisian mission. As soon as Willibrord was assured of the support of Pippin, he set out for Rome to request Pope Sergius I to permit him to undertake the task. The German mission was to proceed under the leadership of Anglo-Saxons and controlled by the Papacy in alliance with the Frankish rulers. That there was some opposition to Willibrord's policy would appear from the rather enigmatic ordination of the Anglo-Saxon Suidbert as regionary bishop of Friesland during Willibrord's absence in Rome; but that the selection of Suidbert in place of Willibrord was due to any objection to Willibrord's desire for the recognition and support of the Papacy seems to be excluded by the fact that it was Wilfrid of York who ordained Suidbert. Suidbert's departure on his mission to the Bructeri left Willibrord in undisturbed possession of the field in Friesland, where he was visited by Wilfrid in 703. After Willibrord's return from Rome the work in Frankish Friesland went on apace. In 695 Willibrord set out again for Rome, where, at the request of Pippin, he was consecrated Archbishop with his see at Utrecht, with full power to organize the Church in Friesland. Before he died, in 739, Frankish Friesland west of the Zuyder-Zee had been fully won for the Christian Church. But all attempts to win over Radbod and independent Friesland had failed. Indeed, the death of Pippin in 714 and the family quarrels which preceded the accession of Charles Martel brought about a reaction. Radbod, in alliance with Neustria, reorganized part of south-western Friesland and drove out the missionaries, burning and destroying the Christian churches. Radbod himself remained a heathen until his life's end. Unfortunately the fine story of St. Wulfram of Sens and Radbod is apocryphal; it relates that Radbod actually approached the baptismal font, but stopped on his way to ask Wulfram whether, if he were baptized, he might hope to meet in heaven his Frisian ancestors, or whether they were in hell. 'Do not deceive thyself,' was Wulfram's reply, 'it is certain that they have received the just sentence of damnation.' Thereupon Radbod drew back from the font, preferring, as he said, to join his own people, wherever they might be, rather than to sit down in the Kingdom of Heaven, with a handful of beggars. There is no evidence whatever that Wulfram of Sens ever preached in Friesland, and, besides, he died in the year 695, which shows that many of the other incidents recorded in the late *Vita S. Wulframmi* must be untrue.

Friesland retained its independence until Radbod's death in 719, and the accession of Charles Martel. Radbod's successor made peace with the Franks, and Willibrord, who had left Friesland in 714, returned to Utrecht to the task of restoring the ruined Church of Frankish Friesland. In this he had the powerful assistance of Wynfrith (Boniface) whom he wished to make his successor. Friesland east of the Zuyder-Zee remained heathen and independent until 734, when the district between the Zuyder-Zee and the Laveke was added to the Frankish Empire. But the aged Willibrord had to leave to younger men the task of christianizing the newly won territory. He died at Epternach in 739 after fifty years of incessant labour, leaving the Christian Church firmly established in western Friesland, and a firm basis for its extension towards the east.

Nor did Willibrord confine his labours to Friesland. Alcuin tells us how as early as 697 he resolved to plant the Faith in Denmark. The terror inspired by Ongend, whom some have identified with the Ongentheow of *Beowulf*, rendered his attempts useless. Driven by a storm to Heligoland, he profaned the holy well of Fosite and with difficulty escaped the vengeance of the infuriated Frisians. Willibrord also prepared the way for an advance of Christianity in central Germany from his monastery at Echternach or Epternach on the

Moselle. Willibrord was by no means the only Anglo-Saxon labouring in Friesland. Anglo-Saxon names are entered in the Calendar of St. Willibrord, written very early in the eighth century. Among his comrades or successors were the above-named Suidbert, chorepiscopus of Utrecht, who, after assisting St. Boniface in his later mission to Friesland, was martyred along with him at Dockum near Leuwarden in 755, and Albert, who came from the school of York (where he had been a pupil of Alcuin) to teach under St. Gregory, abbot of Utrecht. Abbot Gregory, though of Frankish birth, was a pupil of St. Boniface; and under Gregory and Albert Utrecht became the chief centre of Christian learning in Friesland. Yet another Northumbrian was Leofwin or Liafwin who, encouraged by Gregory of Utrecht, went to preach to the Saxons on the Yssel. From England also came one of the most famous of Willibrord's successors, the Northumbrian Willihad. Willihad was another pupil of Alcuin and came to Friesland about 770 with the permission of Alchred of Northumbria. After working for some years at Dockum, Willihad crossed the Laveke and carried the Gospel into far-eastern Friesland, which hitherto had been completely pagan. In 780 he was called by Charles the Great to evangelize the Saxons. Willihad worked at Wignodia with some success until Widukind's rebellion drove him from Saxony. He returned again in 785 to baptize Widukind and to organize the Church in eastern Friesland and adjacent Saxony as bishop of Bremen. Willihad died in 789, and his life was written in the next century by St. Anschar, the apostle of the Danes and Swedes.

Equally famous with St. Willihad in the later history of the Frisian mission is St. Liudger, bishop of Münster, founder of Werden, and missionary to the Saxons. St. Liudger was a Frisian by birth, and he was educated partly under Gregory and Albert at Utrecht, and partly under Alcuin at York, where he spent in all some four years and a half. His expulsion from England because of a feud caused by a Frisian merchant throws an interesting light on Anglo-Frisian relations in the eighth century.

On his return to Friesland Liudger was sent to continue the work begun near Deventer by Leofwin, and to destroy the temples of the false gods throughout Frankish Friesland. Later on he had charge of the church at Dockum. Here, as successor to Willihad, he laboured for seven years until Widukind's rebellion led to a pagan reaction in Friesland and drove Liudger to take refuge for a time at Rome and Monte Cassino. He returned to the work in Friesland in 785. Crossing the Laveke, he preached the Gospel among the newly conquered Frisians east of the Lauwers, and in the island of Heligoland, where he finally destroyed the worship of Fosite. The close of his life was occupied with the foundation of the monastery of Werden on the model of Monte Cassino and the care of the Church among the East Saxons as Bishop of Münster.

Thus the christianization of Friesland, which was begun in 678 by Wilfrid's visit to King Aldgisl, was carried on by a succession of his countrymen or of men trained under them. The evangelization of western and central Friesland, that is to say from the Sinkfal, tributary of the Scheldt, to the Laveke, is associated with the names of Willibrord, Boniface, Eoban, Gregory of Utrecht, and the Northumbrian Albert. The advance across the old boundary of Frankish Friesland and the evangelization of the Saxons (together with the completion of the work begun by Willibrord and Boniface in central Friesland) fell mainly to Leofwin, Willihad, and Liudger, whose task it was to second Charles the Great and to organize the Christian Church among the Saxons, and to prepare the way for a further advance northward in the following century by St. Anschar, a successor of Willihad in the See of Bremen, when the Christian Church of Northumbria, to which Friesland and Saxony owed the faith, was being laid in ruins by the Norsemen.

In this sketch of the history of the evangelization of Friesland, we have had occasion to mention Wynfrith or Boniface among the helpers of St. Willibrord. The conversion of the Frisians was chiefly the work of members of the Church of Northumbria. It is, however, Wessex and southern England which are most closely associated with the beginning of the mission to central Germany, though, as the German mission advanced, helpers were recruited from all parts of England. Indeed, an outstanding feature of the correspondence of St. Boniface and his companions is the very conscious sense of national unity in the face of the separate kingdoms existing in Anglo-Saxon England, which pervades the letters. To take a single example, we find St. Boniface directing an appeal for the prayers of his countrymen for the conversion of the Old Saxons, not to the Churches of Wessex or of the Province of Canterbury, but—to quote his actual words—'immo generaliter omnibus catholicis Deum timentibus de stirpe et prosapia Anglorum'.[1] Anglo-Saxon unity was a reality. As far as the work of the Anglo-Saxon Church in the mission field was concerned they were neither Mercians nor West Saxons nor Northumbrians but *Angli*—English.

The West-Saxon Church was scarcely a generation old when Wynfrith was born of noble parents somewhere about the year 675. The exact place of his birth is unknown, but as the boy was sent by his father to a monastery in Exeter under Abbot Wolfhard, it seems most probable that he was born somewhere in the south-west of England. Exeter was at this time a frontier fortress, and the monastery must have been a very recent foundation. Anyhow it seems to have been inadequately staffed with teachers, so the young Wynfrith soon passed on to the Hampshire monastery of Nursling near Southampton which enjoyed a great reputation under Abbot Winbert, a man who was as famous for administrative ability, scholarship, and penmanship as for his holiness of life. He was a friend of Aldhelm, who was glad to use Winbert's good offices with the king. Aldhelm's influence, whether direct or indirect, is very marked in the earlier letters of St.

[1] Jaffé, *Mon. Mog.* Ep. 39/107.

Boniface. At Nursling Wynfrith spent many years as a Benedictine monk, 'devoted', as his biographer Willibald tells us, 'to the service of the Lord God and laborious perseverance in vigils, and the work of reading the divine word; so that he was imbued not only with the eloquence of the art of grammar and with the pithy modulation of the eloquence of metres, but also with the straight-forward exposition of history and with the triple interpretation of spiritual knowledge [i.e. tropological, allegorical, anagogical] and at last shone so praiseworthily in immense knowledge of the Scriptures that he was even a teacher to others of the traditions of the Fathers and a model master.' The significance of this scheme of education will be dealt with in the next chapter. It affords, however, a valuable glimpse of the extensive range of studies pursued at a comparatively small Anglo-Saxon monastery in the early eighth century. We have in it evidence of the influence of Aldhelm at Nursling, and Aldhelm, bishop of Sherborne and friend of Abbot Winbert, was, as we know from his famous letter to King Gerontius or Geraint, an enthusiastic supporter of the Roman party against the Celts, as well as a devoted adherent of Wilfrid in his struggle with Theodore and the king and bishops of Northumbria. Besides, Wilfrid's personal authority must have been very great in Wessex. Sussex, which he had evangelized, formed part of the diocese of Wynfrith's friend Daniel of Winchester, and Wilfrid himself had been the friend and spiritual father of the wild Cadwalla of Wessex. It was probably Wilfrid's influence that led Cadwalla to seek baptism from Sergius I at Rome. Thus Wynfrith was educated in an atmosphere permeated with the ideals represented by Wilfrid and Aldhelm; and to this may be ascribed that zeal for the enforcement of the discipline and authority of Rome which characterized his whole life, and made him the unwavering protagonist of the rights of the Holy See and its most powerful instrument on the Continent. It is probably to his Nursling period that Boniface's *Latin Grammar* and his work on metres are to be ascribed. The *Riddles* were written in Germany. Wynfrith's fame soon spread beyond Nursling. His ability and scholarship drew scholars from other monasteries, and like Aldhelm he was in special request among nuns of high rank who eagerly sought him as a teacher and as their director in spiritual and temporal affairs. The letters of Boniface show that their sympathy became as necessary to him as his was to them. His reputation and capacity for business led to him being chosen by King Ine of Wessex, on the advice of the abbots of Nursling, Glastonbury, and Tisbury, to lay their case before Brihtwald, archbishop of Canterbury, during a crisis which had arisen within the Church in Wessex. This mission was a great success, and Wynfrith seemed to be marked out for preferment at home, when he decided to devote his life to the conversion of the heathen in Germany. We do not know what led Wynfrith to this decision. All we know is that, in spite of Abbot Winbert's efforts to dissuade him, Wynfrith, with a few companions, sailed from London and landed at Dorstet near Utrecht in the year 716. But he had chosen a most unfavourable time for his mission. Duke Radbod had reconquered Frankish Friesland: he had destroyed the churches and was engaged in a bitter persecution of the Christians. The heathen shrines had been rebuilt and the idols restored. Willibrord had withdrawn to Germany. Wynfrith most courageously ventured to Utrecht and appealed, though vainly, to Radbod to allow him to labour in Friesland. Seeing that it was useless for the time being to remain, he returned to Nursling in 717, more convinced than ever of his vocation, and with clearer views how it was to be realized. Abbot Winbert was dying, and Wynfrith appeared destined to be his successor. But he rejected the proffered honour, and, setting sail again from London, landed near Étaples in the summer or autumn of 718. Instead of proceeding to Friesland, Wynfrith set out for Rome to lay before Pope Gregory II his wish to labour among the heathen of Germany and to obtain his blessing and support.

Once more we have a momentous decision, which was to bind the German mission of the Anglo-Saxon Church closely with the Roman See. Wynfrith's reasons for this step are not known, though they may be guessed. He may have been influenced by the example of St. Willibrord, and his action had the full approval of his diocesan, Daniel of Winchester, who furnished him with a commendatory letter to the Pope. Wynfrith's experience in Friesland must have shown him how important it was to have the authority of the whole Church behind him in his mission, and his training and outlook must have made him eager to have the official authorization of the head of the Church in the struggle against heathendom and heresy. It is noteworthy that Wynfrith, unlike Willibrord, seems to have made no attempt to secure the approval of Charles Martel for his plans, but acted on his own initiative.

At Rome he was most cordially received by Gregory II, who gave him a letter dated 15 May 719, empowering him in the name of the Trinity and the unshaken authority of the blessed Peter, chief of the apostles, to labour among the heathen, to establish discipline, and to administer the sacraments. The date of Gregory's letter is important, for, as Levison has shown, it was now that the name of Boniface was conferred upon Wynfrith by the Pope.

Gregory's letter was a general authorization to evangelize central Europe, east of the Rhine. Boniface's first visit was what Willibald, his biographer, calls 'a tour of inspection'. Proceeding from Rome, via Lombardy, he passed through Bavaria and Thuringia on his way to Franconia. The situation in these lands was difficult and critical. With the increasing weakness of the Merovingian Empire since the days of Dagobert, the Frankish Church had lost whatever influence it ever possessed over the peoples of central and southern Germany, who had been left dependent for the most part on the zeal and devotion of wandering missionaries of Irish or Frankish birth, such as St. Rupert, St. Kilian of Würzburg, St. Emmeran, St. Corbinian, and others. Bavaria had been a well-organized Christian land, but now clergy and people were demoralized. Thuringia had been partially evangelized by the disciples of St. Columba, but paganism had returned, so that the whole land was either totally or semi-heathen. Moreover, where Christianity survived it was often of a non-Roman type: Celtic and other nonconformist practices were rife.

From Thuringia Boniface passed on to Franconia, where he learnt of the death of Duke Radbod. The removal of its most powerful enemy left the way free for the advance of Christianity in Friesland, and Boniface believed himself to be divinely called to assist St. Willibrord, for a time at least. He spent three years, 719–22, helping Willibrord to restore and reorganize the ruined and persecuted Church in Friesland. It was but natural that St. Willibrord should have been most anxious for Boniface to succeed him as bishop of Utrecht. But Boniface steadfastly refused, pleading that he was bound to the nations of Germany by Gregory's commission. 'Most holy bishop', was his reply '... I brought to the nations of Germany the charge of blessed Pope Gregory ... Without the decree of the apostolic see, and without its commission and authentic command, I dare not undertake a rank so distinguished and sublime.' Willibrord was compelled to let him go, and in 723 Boniface left Friesland for Amanaburch in Hesse, and for the great work of his life, the evangelization of the peoples of central Germany, which was to lead to the reorganization and reformation of the whole Frankish Church and the restoration of the authority and discipline of the Roman Church over a great part of western Europe.

Boniface's choice of Hesse was probably suggested by its position. Part of the Frankish Empire, Hesse lay near the borders of the Saxons, and the conversion of the Saxons, the continental kinsmen of the Anglo-Saxons, was the darling ambition of Boniface's life, though he was not destined to achieve it. Hesse had been utterly neglected by the Bishop of Mainz, in whose sphere of influence it lay. At Amanaburch (Amoneburg) on the river Ohm Boniface found two chieftains, Dettic and Deorwulf, who worshipped idols though they called themselves Christians. 'The Saint', Willibald tells us, 'summoned them from the sacrilegious worship of idols, which they wrongfully practised under the name of Christianity; and withdrew a very great multitude of people . . . from heathenism.' Amoneburg was chosen by Boniface as his base of operations, and from here Christianity spread throughout Hesse to the borders of Saxony. So great was the success of the missionaries that Boniface sent one of his countrymen called Binna with full reports to Pope Gregory II. The Pope at once grasped the importance of the work for the future of the Roman Church, and summoned Boniface to Rome. After undergoing a thorough examination of his doctrinal views, Boniface was consecrated regionary bishop of Germany on St. Andrew's Day 723. Before returning to Germany Boniface bound himself by a solemn oath of fealty to the Papacy—an oath which he faithfully kept until death.

Armed with the full authority of the Holy See and provided with commendatory letters from the Pope to Charles Martel and to the clergy and laity, Boniface returned to Germany. He seems to have met Charles for the first time when he delivered to him the letter of Gregory II. The attitude of Charles to Boniface is in contrast with his relations to St. Willibrord, whom he generously supported. Boniface's relations with the Papacy may have been the reason for Charles's coolness. At all events Charles gave Boniface a letter of protection, and allowed him to return to Hesse, without, however, making any reference to the papal commission of Boniface. In spite of the great advance made by Christianity in Hesse, heathenism was still far from being conquered. It was now that Boniface determined to strike a decisive blow against the old religion. With his own hands he hewed down the holy oak of Gaismar, sacred to Thor, before an assembled crowd, and built with its timber a wooden oratory, which he dedicated to St. Peter. The old religion in Hesse fell with the destruction of the national shrine.

From Hesse Boniface passed on into Thuringia, where there was the same mixture of heathenism and Christianity as in Hesse. The Church was in a state of utter disorder and heretical practices were rampant. Boniface summoned the Thuringian nobles to meet him and entreated them to return to the Christian Faith which they had once held but in their ignorance had deserted. The greatest difficulties of Boniface came from heretical teachers. Willibald mentions the names of four of these—Torchtwine, Berchthere, Eanbercht, and Hunred—and describes them as fornicators and adulterers, which probably means that they did not observe the Roman rule of the celibacy of the clergy, and were married priests. The names of these four appear to be Anglo-Saxon, but who they were it is not easy to say. It has been suggested that they were members of an Anglo-Saxon mission from Willibrord's monastery of Echternach, who had lapsed from the Faith. But there does not seem to be sufficient evidence for this. Possibly they were Anglo-Saxon members of the Celtic Church who had left Northumbria for Germany after Whitby. This, however, is nothing more than a conjecture. What is clear is that Boniface had to win again in Germany and the Frankish Empire generally the victory over the remnants of the Celtic Church on the Continent which had been won in 664 at Whitby by St. Wilfrid and the Roman party in England. In Thuringia, as in Hesse, the devotion and enthusiasm of St. Boniface, whose authority was supported by repeated letters from Rome, won the day, and the multitude of believers increased.

'The report of his holy preaching was so spread abroad, and increased to such a degree, that already his fame resounded through the greatest part of Europe. And from the parts of Britain an exceeding great multitude of the congregation of the servants of God had come unto him: readers and writers also, and men learned in other arts. Of these a very great number put themselves under the instruction of his rule, and in very many places summoned the people from the profane error of heathenism. And some in the province of the Hessians, and others in Thuringia, widely dispersed among the people, preached the word of God to the country districts and villages.'[1]

Churches were built and a monastery at Ohrdruf near Erfurt, which served as a base of operations for Thuringia. The result of almost ten years of continuous toil (723-32) was the creation in Hesse and Thuringia of a new Christian Church on a purely Roman model, which in devotion, orthodoxy, and discipline presented a model to the rest of the Frankish Empire.

In 732 Boniface had reached for the third time a turning-point in his life. Had he been left to his own choice there can be little doubt that he would now have felt himself free to begin what he looked forward to as the great task of his life, the evangelization of the Saxons, but the Papacy had other work for the great Anglo-Saxon—nothing less than the reorganization of the Churches of Bavaria and Alamannia and the inauguration of a reformation of the whole Frankish Church, which should culminate in the restoration of the lost authority of the See of Rome over the Western Church, in close association with the Frankish monarchy.

The year 732 was one of the most critical in European history. The strength of the Papacy was being exhausted in a renewed struggle with the eastern emperors in the Iconoclast Controversy. The Moors had conquered Spain and crossed the Pyrenees into southern Gaul. 'The victorious Saracen had overrun the provinces of

[1] *Willibald*, c. 6.

Aquitaine ... and his detachments overspread the kingdom of Burgundy as far as the well-known cities of Lyons and Besançon.' Though modern historians are inclined to think that Gibbon exaggerates when he says, 'Perhaps the interpretation of the Koran would now be taught in the schools of Oxford, and her pulpits might demonstrate to a circumcized people the sanctity and truth of the revelation of Mahomet,' there can be no doubt that Charles Martel's victory of Poitiers saved Christian France from a terrible calamity. In the face of such events we can imagine the sense of relief and hope which the news of the victorious advance of Roman Christianity under its Anglo-Saxon leaders in the lands east of the Rhine must have brought to the anxious heads of the Church at Rome. The winning of Friesland and the Germanic tribes east of the Rhine and the re-establishment of some real authority over the Frankish Church meant immediate compensation for the loss of Spain, and made the future of Catholicism in Europe secure.

In 731 Gregory II died, but in his successor, Gregory III, Boniface found an equally firm supporter. The new Pope at once assured Boniface of his friendship, bestowed upon him the rank of regionary archbishop with authority to ordain bishops, and the gift of the pallium as a symbol of his legatine authority. In virtue of his new position, Boniface determined to visit Bavaria. But the time was not yet quite propitious for a reorganization of the Bavarian Church. Duke Hugobert was too suspicious of the Frankish archbishop to allow him a free hand, and all that Boniface was able to do on this occasion was to inspect the Bavarian churches, condemn and cut off certain schismatics, and prepare the way for the future. In 738 Boniface, now sixty years of age, visited Rome for the third time. His chief object would seem to have been to gain the Pope's permission to proceed with the evangelization of the Saxons. But Gregory, while according a general approval to the missionary plans of Boniface, created him Papal Vicar and plenipotentiary for all Germany, and sent him back to complete the organization and reformation of the Church throughout South Germany and Alamannia. The Church in Alamannia (where Pirmin had been labouring at Reichenau) had to wait, but with the hearty co-operation of the new duke, Odilo, Boniface now proceeded with the much-needed reform of the Bavarian Church. Bavaria was divided into four bishoprics, Salzburg, Freising, Regensburg, and Passau; monasteries were founded, national synods established, and the Church purged from heresy and schism whether of Celtic or Teutonic origin. In 741 a fifth bishopric was founded, at Eichstätt. The first bishop of Eichstätt was the Anglo-Saxon Willibald, a relative of Boniface, and an alumnus of the Hampshire monastery of Bishops Waltham. The Church in Bavaria was now Catholic in its discipline and organization.

Meantime the Church of Hesse and Thuringia had been organized on the Roman model. The see of Büraburg, near Fritzlar, was established for Hesse with the

Anglo-Saxon Witta as its bishop; the See of Würzburg (the scene of the labours of the Irish St. Killian) for southern Thuringia with Burchard of Malmesbury as its bishop; and the see of Erfurt for northern Thuringia.

Thus by the year 741 the Anglo-Saxon Church, in close co-operation with the Papacy, but without the help of the Carolings, had established Christianity on a firm basis throughout Hesse and Thuringia and reorganized the decadent Church of Bavaria. Throughout central Germany, east of the Rhine, the authority of the Papal See had become a reality and Roman standards of faith, discipline, and organization were supreme. Everywhere there was evidence of a vigorous spiritual and intellectual life in striking contrast with the moral torpor, mental stagnation, and relaxed discipline which marked the remainder of the Frankish Church. The question was whether the reform movement was to spread westwards to Austrasia and Neustria. Here everything depended on the attitude of the Frankish sovereign. In 741 Charles Martel died. His death opened the way for a union between Church and State such as had not hitherto existed in the Frankish Empire.

Charles Martel was succeeded by Carloman in Austrasia and by Pippin in Neustria. Their education at St. Denys had made both of the new rulers anxious for the reform of the Frankish Church—but the movement first began in Austrasia. On his accession Carloman summoned Boniface and asked him to call a synod of the Austrasian Church, promising his help to correct and amend the ecclesiastical discipline which had been trampled upon and dissipated for not less than sixty or seventy years. This synod, which met in 742 and included the greater nobles as well as ecclesiastics, met under the legatine authority of Archbishop Boniface. Its decisions provided for annual synods of the Austrasian Church, enforced the authority of bishops over presbyters, prohibited clerical concubinage, put down idolatrous and schismatical practices, and in general enforced the ecclesiastical canons, which now became part of the law of the land. Carloman's example was followed by Pippin of Neustria at the Council of Soissons in 744—which was followed by a joint synod of Austrasia and Neustria, held in 745 under the presidency of Boniface. The results may be summed up in the words of a famous Roman Catholic historian, Professor Kurth of Liège, who affirms that 'the religious regeneration which resulted from Boniface's action throughout the Frankish Empire is worthy of comparison with the religious regeneration of the universal Church which resulted from the Council of Trent.' A seal was set upon the theocratic union which was to unite the Carolings with the Roman Church, when Boniface as papal legate, following the Anglo-Saxon custom, anointed Pippin king of the Franks in A.D. 752.

We have now seen how the interposition of the Anglo-Saxon Church in the continental missions to Friesland and central Germany prepared the way for the restoration of the weakened or lost authority of the Papacy, not only over the newly evangelized districts of Friesland and Hesse and Thuringia, but over Bavaria, Austrasia,

THE ANGLO-SAXONS ON THE CONTINENT 63

and the whole Carolingian Empire, and paved the way for that alliance between the Empire and the Papacy which, under the name of the Holy Roman Empire, was to be fraught with such tremendous results for the history of both Church and State in the Middle Ages. The rest of the life of Boniface may be briefly summed up. In 743 he became archbishop of Mainz. He succeeded Gerulius, who had been deposed from his see partly because like Chaucer's monk he was a great hunter, but more especially because like Spencer of Norwich he was a great warrior and had been guilty of homicide. The next year, 744, saw the foundation of Fulda, a place inseparably connected with the name of Boniface, as well as with the history of learning and religion in Carolingian Germany. Here Boniface, with his friend Leoba, was buried; and here, later, a famous teacher of the Church, Hrabanus Maurus, taught and prayed. Sturmi, the first abbot of Fulda, was brought as a boy by Boniface from Bavaria and placed under the Anglo-Saxon Wigbert at Fritzlar. Later on Boniface sent him to study the Benedictine Rule at Monte Cassino. Fulda became a Monte Cassino for Germany, and before Sturmi's death it contained 400 monks.

Boniface was now growing infirm in body, but not in purpose. In 753, with the permission of the Pope and of Pippin, he was allowed to name Lull of Malmesbury as his successor in the See of Mainz. Set free at last from the work of organizing and superintending the Church, the aged Boniface, with indomitable courage, set out on what he felt was to be his last mission to the heathen of

Friesland. Passing down the Rhine, and crossing the Zuyder Zee, Boniface, accompanied by his countryman Bishop Eoban and some forty or fifty companions, encamped at Dockum near Leuwarden to await the arrival of the candidates for confirmation. But instead of the catechumens came a raging throng of heathen Frisians, who butchered the saint and his companions on 4 June 755. It was a fitting death for one who had been a warrior all his life, and the one for which he had longed above all others.

Hitherto we have confined our attention almost exclusively to the life of Boniface himself. But the evangelization of central Germany was not the work of one man. Boniface had the assistance of large numbers of his countrymen. Willibald speaks of the multitude of readers, and writers, and men skilled in various arts who came to him from Britain. The names of most of these are unknown, and I have time only for a few brief notes on some of the more important of the names which have come down.

It should be observed that Boniface drew his helpers almost without exception from the monasteries of Kent and Wessex, whereas the Frisian mission was in the main the work of the Northumbrian Church, which, at a later date, lent powerful assistance to Germany from its school of York.

Lull is perhaps the most famous among the helpers of St. Boniface. Born of a good family, Lull was educated at Malmesbury and preserved a great admiration for Aldhelm. Later on he may have studied under Boniface at Nursling. As a young man he visited Rome, but the call of Boniface brought him to Germany. Boniface made him his archdeacon, and finally chorepiscopus of Mainz and his successor. The qualities which had recommended him to St. Boniface made him a vigorous and capable ruler of the Church, though his zeal for the rights of his see brought him into a lamentable quarrel with Abbot Sturmi of Fulda, the greatest of Boniface's German disciples. Lull was a man of scholarly tastes and an eager collector of books for the German libraries, as witness his frequent requests for the works of Bede. On the other hand, there is no evidence that he showed any disposition to carry out the task bequeathed by St. Boniface, of extending the frontiers of Christianity to the east and north. From Malmesbury probably came Burchard, the first bishop of Würzburg, and the trusted presbyter, Deneheard. Glastonbury sent the presbyter Wiehtberht, who tells us of the warm welcome which he and his companions received from St. Boniface. But deserving of special mention among the Anglo-Saxon assistants of St. Boniface are Willibald, Wunibald, and their sister Walburgis or Walpurgis. St. Willibald (not to be confounded with the biographer of St. Boniface) was the first bishop of Eichstädt in Bavaria, and one of the most famous of Anglo-Saxon travellers. The lives of both brothers were written by an Anglo-Saxon nun of Heidenheim. From these lives we learn that they were born about 700, and were educated at Bishops Waltham near Eastleigh in Hants. About 720 they sailed from the mouth of the Hampshire river Hamble (accompanied by their father) for Rome. Their father died on the road. Wunibald decided to remain in Rome, but Willibald set sail for the East, via Sicily, and spent seven years in travelling throughout the Holy Land. Returning at last to Italy, he spent the next ten years at Monte Cassino. At the request of Pope Gregory III, he joined Boniface in Germany and was ordained bishop of Eichstädt in 741. Wunibald had also entered Monte Cassino, but, on the invitation of St. Boniface, he proceeded to Thuringia. When his brother Willibald became bishop, Wunibald became abbot of the double monastery of Heidenheim, to which their sister Walpurgis had been invited. Walpurgis had been educated at Wimborne under Abbess Tetta and seems to have come out to Germany with Leoba and others in 748. In 750 Walpurgis became abbess of Heidenheim, where she died in 780. Walpurgis was canonized on 1 May, and hence the connexion of this gentle Hampshire lady with the orgies of Walpurgis-Nacht.

The most beloved of all Boniface's helpers was Leoba, abbess of Bischopsheim, who was buried by his side. Leoba (Leobgyth) was educated under the cultured and energetic Abbess Eadburg in the abbey of St. Mary Thanet. Her abbess was one of the most intimate correspondents of St. Boniface. From Thanet Leoba passed under the sterner rule of Abbess Tetta of Wimborne (a sister of Ine of Wessex) of whom she has left a realistic picture. Her letters show a mastery of the Latin language that most modern graduates might envy, though she apologizes for her rustic style, and asks Boniface to send her letters of his own as a standard. She tells St. Boniface that she had learned the art of verse-making from Eadburga, and sends him four lines, strongly reminiscent of Aldhelm, as a specimen of her skill. Her biographer speaks of her knowledge of the Scriptures and the Fathers, to which she added an interest in chronology and Canon Law. Ebert has suggested that it was to her that Boniface dedicated his *Riddles*. But Leoba was no mere blue-stocking of the eighth century. She combined an unusually lovable and attractive disposition with remarkable practical qualities. She willingly obeyed Boniface's summons to Germany, and with her went Chunihilt, Chunitrud, and Thecla—all of whom were skilled in the liberal arts and were established as heads of monastic institutions throughout Germany. Leoba was appointed to Bischopsheim, where a large number of religious women had been collected. When Boniface was starting on his last journey to Friesland he sent for Leoba and begged her not to desert the land of her pilgrimage. He commended her to Lull, and expressed the wish that, after her death, her bones should be laid in the same tomb with his own.

Even more important to the student of Anglo-Saxon history and literature are the letters which passed between the Anglo-Saxons on the Continent and the members of the Church at home in England. To deal with them adequately would require at least another lecture, and all one can hope to do is to call attention to some of the very valuable evidence which they afford of the level of moral and intellectual achievement attained by the Anglo-Saxon Church throughout all parts of England just about the time to which the composition of the major portion of Anglo-Saxon poetry is usually ascribed. We all know more or less of famous Anglo-Saxon schools like Canterbury, York, Wearmouth and Jarrow, and even Malmesbury and perhaps Glastonbury, but it is with something of surprise that we learn from the *Monumenta Moguntina*, the *Monumenta Alcuiniana*, and the authentic *Vitae Sanctorum* that many otherwise unknown monasteries of both men and women combined the pursuit of the religious life with a keen interest in sacred and secular learning and the propagation of the Faith among their continental kinsmen. Neither Bede nor the Chronicle mentions Nursling, yet Nursling, at the beginning of the eighth century, was the scene of a very vigorous intellectual life which attracted scholars from neighbouring schools. Its abbot, Wynbert, was not merely a promoter of the liberal arts of the school of Aldhelm, but an artist in penmanship whose manuscript of the six prophets, written in clear and separate letters, excited the longing of Boniface in a land where he could not procure such a book. Not far from Nursling was Bishops Waltham, which produced two saints and scholars in St. Willibald of Eichstädt and St. Wunibald of Heidenheim. Away in the west was Exeter, which was Boniface's first school, and Tisbury in Wiltshire had, through its abbot, at least some share in his career.

A notable feature of the correspondence is the light thrown upon the part played by women in the religious and intellectual life of the late seventh and eighth centuries. St. Hilda of Whitby was far from being unique. The letters of Boniface and Lull show that Anglo-Saxon women, many of them of royal and noble birth, played a scarcely less important part than men in the promotion of learning as well as religion, and had attained a degree of culture rare among women until comparatively recent times. Among the most faithful friends of St. Boniface was Eadburga, abbess of Thanet, who, like Hildelida of Barking, while interested in the purgatorial visions of the Monk of Wenlock, was, at the same time, a lady mighty in the Scriptures, erudite in the Fathers, mistress of the art of Latin verse composition, and so skilled in penmanship that she was able to produce for St. Boniface a manuscript of the *Epistles of St. Peter* in letters of gold. Abbess Eangyth, though she bemoans her rustic and unpolished style, lays bare her heart to Boniface in a letter of plangent eloquence, replete with scriptural allusions, with a storm-piece reminiscent of parts of the *Andreas*. Abbess Tetta of Wimborne, although lacking the charm of Leoba, appears to have ruled with great and royal capacity a double-monastery which, no doubt, afforded full scope for her not altogether winsome disposition. Of Abbess Bugga, daughter of Eangyth, of whom Boniface declares that she is 'in the hope of Christ to be preferred to all others of feminine sex,' we know that she was an accomplished Latin scholar, who busied herself in providing books, such as the *Passiones Martyrum*, for Boniface, and was, at the same time, skilled in the more feminine craft of needlework. To these accomplishments she joined a deeply religious nature and a profound devotion to St. Boniface which lasted until death.

Besides women like these, we meet in the letters bishops such as Boniface's faithful friend, Daniel of Winchester, a Nestor in counsel which was not always taken, and, in spite of his holy life, charged by some of his colleagues with remissness in baptizing infants; Pechthelm of Whitern, an alumnus of Malmesbury, consulted by Boniface on a troublesome point in the Canon Law regarding marriage; and Milret of Worcester, expressing to Lull his grief at the martyrdom of St. Boniface, and regretting his inability to send him a liturgy on parchment of stained purple, because it had been borrowed by Bishop Cuthbert. Nothelm of Canterbury is asked by Boniface for the Augustine Interrogations, Abbot Dudda for works on the Epistles of St. Paul and other useful works, Hwaetberht and Cuthbert (as well as others) of Wearmouth and Jarrow, for the works of Bede, whom Boniface terms the candle of the Church. Successive archbishops of Canterbury and York appear in the letters, sometimes as participators in mutual prayer unions with the Church in Germany, and sometimes receiving admonition and counsel from Boniface, Lull, or Alcuin, regarding disorders in the Anglo-Saxon Church. Kings, too, have their place. Boniface's famous letter to Aethilbald of Mercia is a fearless and fearful indictment of the personal character of the king and of the corruptions of the times. Alchred of Northumbria, Aethelbert II of Kent, and Cynewulf of Wessex (famous through the vivid story of his death told in the Anglo-Saxon Chronicle) are among the sovereigns who ask for the prayers of St. Boniface.

The subject is far from being exhausted, but enough has been said to suggest the interest and value of the study of the letters to the student of Anglo-Saxon England during the century in which the Church in Northumbria was distressed by civil war and disaster. Of fourteen kings of Northumbria from 705 not one died in peaceful possession of his throne. Mercia was engaged under two able kings, Aethilbald and Offa, in making itself supreme, and extending its power over Kent and Wessex, until the house of Offa perished and with it the greatness of Mercia, and, for a time, the greatness of Anglo-Saxon England.

III

ANGLO-SAXON ENGLAND AND THE TRANSMISSION OF ANCIENT CULTURE

THE amalgamation of Celtic and Roman Christianity in England in the second half of the seventh century and the Anglo-Saxon missions to Friesland and Germany, together with the subsequent reformation of the Frankish Church, were events which have an intimate bearing upon one of the most important phenomena in history—the transmission of the culture of the ancient world to medieval and modern times.

But lest there should be any suspicion that my special studies and interests are leading me, unconsciously perhaps, to attach an exaggerated importance to the part played by the Celts and Anglo-Saxons in the history of human culture, it may be well at the outset to quote the words of Eduard Norden, whose commanding position among modern classical scholars precludes any thought of bias. Discussing the relative importance of the Barbarians and the Christian Church as mediators of Graeco-Roman culture, Norden assigns the more effective and decisive role to the Christian Church; since, he says, it was through Christianity that ancient learning was transmitted to the Barbarians and it was Christianity which provided the foundation of ancient literature upon which they erected their own national cultures. 'There were', he adds, 'in the main three factors working in this direction, the efforts of Cassiodorus, the Irish, and the Anglo-Saxons.'[1] Elsewhere Norden says: 'It is impossible for the classical scholar to exaggerate the significance of the part played by the Irish in the work of preserving classical literature.'[2]

The average classical scholar, unless he be a man of the calibre of a Mommsen or a Norden, a Bury or a Dill, has an instinctive shrinking from medieval studies. Medievalism is for him the antithesis of all that he has been taught to value. In classical literature he finds the emphasis laid upon human freedom, individualism, and personality; medievalism presents him with dogma in place of freedom; an all-embracing authority for individualism; and anonymity for personality. In the classics he finds beauty, form, and regulated, cultivated taste; in medieval literature he finds neglect of form and external beauty; the emphasis is upon the content, the matter, the spirit—the expression is too often chaotic. The classics reflect a permanent, cheerful world full of sunshine and light, in which man is encouraged to get as much pleasure as he can from life, and to gratify to the full his capacity for enjoyment, regulated as far as may be by the dictates of reason and good taste. If Acheron exists it is kept discreetly in the background, and Cerberus is chained. The medieval world, on the other hand, is darkened by the shadow of the Last Judgement: it is but a transitory habitation for exiles

[1] *Die Antike Kunstprosa*, ii. 663.   [2] Ibid. 667.

from the heavenly fatherland. Hell is always in the foreground and the devil is unchained. Like the classical world it has its athletes; but the athletes of the Middle Ages are the athletes of the soul. The world of the classics is an exclusive world: the barbarians lie beyond its pale. The newer Christian world presented a universalism in which, to quote the words of St. Paul, there was to be 'neither Jew nor Greek, bond nor free, but Christ [was to] be all and in all'.

Such, in quite general terms, is the contrast between the world of the classics and that of the Middle Ages. Yet the difference was not really so great as it might at first appear, for there is evidence that in many directions what are sometimes regarded as typical features of medievalism are rooted in the pre-Christian age. Thus the dogmas and absolute authority claimed by the medieval Church have their counterpart in the dogmas and *ipse dixits* of the philosophical schools of Greece and Rome. There were many in the classical age who took a less cheerful view of life than Horace. There is not much to choose between the Platonic doctrine of the world as a prison-house in which humanity is languishing, and the doctrine of the Christian hymn:

> 'Earth is a desert drear
> Heaven is my home.'

Nor is the transition from $\dot{\alpha}\theta\lambda\eta\tau\alpha\grave{\iota}\ \tau\hat{\omega}\nu\ \pi\alpha\theta\hat{\omega}\nu$ like Dio, Seneca, and Epictetus to St. Paul difficult. The universalism of the Christian Church was anticipated by Hellenism, in which the earlier individualism and

THE TRANSMISSION OF ANCIENT CULTURE

aristocratic exclusiveness of the city states has been replaced by the more popular gospel proclaimed from end to end of the Roman Empire by the wandering preachers of Stoicism and other religio-philosophic cults. There are also signs in the Hellenistic and following eras that the classical emphasis upon the supreme value of beauty and outward form is changing—markedly so in the teaching of a man like Epictetus—to emphasis upon the content, though not yet at the expense of the form. The truth is that in the centuries immediately preceding the fall of the Roman Empire a good deal of what we call medievalism was already in the air. Apart altogether from any influence of Christianity, Graeco-Roman culture was dying with the society which gave it birth. That it did not perish, it owes mainly to the agency of the two factors who are often credited with its destruction, the Christian Church and the Barbarians.

It would, however, be a grave mistake to credit the Church or the Barbarians with a serious interest in Graeco-Roman literature and art; still less had they any conscious concern for their preservation. From the fifth century onward, the interest of the Church in literature and the arts was due solely to the fact that to study the Scriptures and to instruct the faithful it was necessary for the clergy to be able to read, and perhaps write, and that some further knowledge of the arts, particularly of music, was required to conduct the various services of the Church in an adequate manner. This had not always been so: in the days of the great Apologists and during the struggle with heretical sects a more intimate acquaintance with classical literature and philosophy had been necessary; but with the death of Julian and the subsequent decline in paganism the victorious Church, with but few exceptions, had seen less and less reason to occupy itself with ancient learning, whose pagan content caused it to be regarded as a menace rather than a support to the new Faith.

But though Tertullian called upon the Church to shun the temptations presented by the culture of the pagan world and to renounce its learning as an enemy of the soul, there were profounder minds who took a different view. St. Clement of Alexandria and Origen realized the necessity of the Church's utilizing all that was best in ancient culture in the exposition of the Christian Faith, and had proved its value in their works which had an authoritative value in both East and West. Their motto was that of St. Paul, 'Prove all things, and hold fast that which is good', and they justified their practice by an allegorical interpretation of the Mosaic story how the Israelites on departing from Egypt were told by God to borrow ornaments and vessels from the Egyptians. For the Christian scholars the liberal arts—the trivium and quadrivium—were the ornaments and vessels of the Egyptians, and to plunder the Egyptians, or to use pagan culture in the service of the Church, became the watchword of the more liberal school of medieval Christian scholars. Or to employ another favourite figure—the liberal arts became the slave girl of Deut. xxi. 11-12, whom the Israelite might appropriate, if he shaved her hair and cut her nails. In spite of a good many contradictions in word, if not in practice, the example of Clement and Origen was that followed by the two great Doctors of the Western Church, Jerome and Augustine, while the third great Doctor of the West, St. Gregory, followed Tertullian.

While the Roman Empire lasted and secular education was maintained in the imperial schools, the attitude of the authorities of the Church, though of steadily growing importance, was not yet vital to ancient culture.

A Tertullian or a Cassian might declaim against the insidious temptations offered to the Christian by the study of profane literature and art; yet so long as the imperial schools were open and frequented by the laity, the old traditional learning was available for laity and clergy alike and lived on secure.

But when the Barbarian invasions and the consequent fall of the Western Empire brought in their train the ruin of the imperial system of education, the Christian Church became the sole arbitress and controller of education, and her policy in the matter became decisive for the destiny of ancient letters. The protection afforded to learning by Theodoric the Great and his successor delayed the ruin of culture in Italy, and as late as the first half of the sixth century men like Ennodius, Cassiodorus, and Boethius—the last of the Romans— added a certain lustre to the schools of Italy. But it was the glow of the setting sun, and not of the dawn. Learning and the Fine Arts shared in the general disintegration which befell Italy during the late sixth and seventh centuries, when the Lombards overran the country, and the wretched populace (augmented in the seventh century by the arrival of multitudes of fugitives from Syria, Egypt, and Africa, fleeing before the advance of the Moslems) were scourged and decimated by the plagues of war, pestilence, famine, and religious strife.

Nor were the prospects for the study of the liberal arts in sixth-century Gaul much brighter. Indeed they were even worse. The Celts of Gaul had assimilated the culture and civilization of their Roman conquerors with an eagerness and thoroughness unsurpassed by any other people in the Empire. By the fourth century the fame of the schools of Gaul had penetrated to the most distant provinces. No land had produced so many masters of ornate rhetoric, or possessed more famous schools overflowing with students of all the arts of the trivium and quadrivium. This happy state of affairs, however, was not to last. The seeds of decay, already apparent in so typical a writer as Ausonius, are in vigorous growth in the fifth century in Sidonius Apollinaris and his circle. Sidonius and his correspondents would seem to have lost all contact with the realities of the iron age in which they lived. For them, literature, philosophy, and eloquence have ceased to be more than pastimes and an esoteric cult serving to differentiate its votaries from the vulgar. Polished, courtly, dilettanti, they were utterly unfitted in character and outlook to be the guardians of ancient learning. Nowhere do they appear to have had any adequate notion of the value of the heritage which was in their keeping, much less any thought of transmitting it unimpaired or augmented to their Barbarian contemporaries.

The State schools of Gaul continued to exist during the first quarter of the fifth century, or possibly a little longer in centres of learning like Bordeaux, Lyons, and Narbonne. But the destruction of the Roman state organization entailed the cessation of the demand for officials trained in the civic ideal of ancient education, and as the century advanced schools maintained at the public expense became rarer and rarer, and in the end education was left either to private enterprise or to the Church.

How far, then, was the place left vacant by the decay of the imperial schools filled during the sixth century by monastic and episcopal schools? For those whose memories are full of records of the services of the monks in the West, not only to religion but to learning, there will be but one answer. Of course, you will say, the task which dropped from the nerveless grasp of the dying Empire was taken up and maintained with enthusiasm by the Church—particularly in the monastic schools. Yet at this point it may be well to recall the words of Mabillon,[1] who will not be suspected of any anti-monastic bias.

'It is', says the great Benedictine, 'an illusion of certain writers of the previous century that the monasteries were

[1] *Traité des ét. mon.* i. 7.

founded primarily to serve as schools and colleges in which the teaching of the humane sciences became a profession. But what really gave birth to these holy institutions was the passion for virtue and for separation from the world—scorn for the secular life and its corruptions.'

For the founders of western monasticism there was a chasm between pagan culture and Christian ideals. 'Hearts vowed to Christ', cried St. Paulinus of Nola, 'have no welcome for the goddesses of song; they are barred to Apollo. . . . Another force, a mightier God, subdues my soul.' These words of St. Paulinus are typical of the general attitude of the Church in Gaul to ancient learning. In general, it followed the tradition of Tertullian rather than that of Origen and Augustine. Sulpicius Severus, in the preface to his life of St. Martin, declares that 'the kingdom of God is not in eloquence, but in faith', and demands, 'what good will it do posterity to study the philosophy of Socrates or to read the battles of Hector?'[1] St. Cassian is even more explicit. In one of his *colloquies* he represents a monk asking Abbot Nestor how to get rid of the pagan memories which haunt him even when he is singing the Psalms. He is told to substitute the reading of the Holy Scriptures and meditations for the study of profane authors. Elsewhere Cassian declares that 'the syllogisms of dialectic and Ciceronian eloquence are unworthy of the simple truths of the faith'.[2]

This suspicious attitude continued, even when there

[1] *Vita Mart.*
[2] *Inst.* xii. 19.

THE TRANSMISSION OF ANCIENT CULTURE

was little fear of any pagan revival. A most careful examination of all the available evidence has led M. Roger to sum up the situation in the seventh century as follows:

'It seemed that the Faith could suffice with a very elementary education, and that all the clergy required was to be able to read and write, and to know a little singing. The study of the scriptures had suffered severely from the abandonment of classical culture. To understand the scriptures they were content to read and reproduce the Fathers—either resigning themselves to not grasping everything, or even confining themselves to learning and reciting the psalms.'

It is eloquent of the condition of learning in Gaul in the sixth century that we do not possess a single classical manuscript which can be shown to have been copied in Gaul at this date. The scribes confined their labours entirely to religious texts.

In Italy in the first half of the sixth century a fair prospect seemed to be opening for the retention of the study of the liberal arts in the service of the Church. The programme of Christian education outlined by St. Augustine in his *De Doctrina Christiana* formed the basis of the scheme of studies prescribed by Cassiodorus for the monks of the Monastery of Viviers founded by him in 540.

Born of a noble and wealthy family of Bruttium, Cassiodorus had been the trusted servant and minister of Odoacer, Theodoric the Great, and their successors. On the fall of the Ostrogothic kingdom, Cassiodorus, then a man of seventy, retired from public life to his ancestral estates, where he founded the monastery of Viviers, declaring that it was a nobler thing to serve Christ than to possess the kingdoms of the earth.

Here, on a site overlooking the sea, with fish-ponds and beautiful gardens, his monks were presented with an ideal of the ascetic life very different from that of Cassian or the contemporary St. Benedict. Cassiodorus aimed at making the monastery not merely a centre of moral discipline but also a centre of enlightenment, in which ancient learning might be cultivated in the service of the Christian Faith and preserved from the imminent risk of perishing amid the barbarism which supervened upon the destruction of the kingdom of Theodoric. Cassiodorus set forth his scheme of studies in his great work, the *Institutiones Divinarum et Secularium Lectionum* in two books, the first dealing with sacred and the second with profane literature. There he declares that the sole object of monastic studies should be the perfect understanding of the Holy Scriptures, and accordingly he prescribes the careful reading of the sacred texts, the works of the Fathers, and the Christian historians. He urges the study of the geography of the Holy Land, and the necessity of knowing the arts of grammar, rhetoric, dialectic, arithmetic, music, and geometry. 'The knowledge of all the arts is useful to the student of scripture, and must not be shunned,' he declares. For this reason he gives us in the second book of the *Institutions* a classification of the liberal arts based probably on Martianus Capella. Here we have the classification of humane studies (which was to remain for the schools of the Middle Ages) into the Trivium (grammar, rhetoric, and dialectic) and the Quadrivium embracing arithmetic, geometry, music, and astronomy. Throughout the *Institutions*, Cassiodorus quotes frequently from profane authors, but he nowhere recommends the reading of ancient poetry.

The programme of sacred studies combined with the humanities outlined by Cassiodorus was destined, though not immediately, to have a profound influence upon the course of monasticism in the Middle Ages; and the modern student of the classics is deeply indebted to this great collector of ancient manuscripts who established a scriptorium at Viviers in which the library was replenished and enlarged by skilled copyists under his personal direction.

But Cassiodorus was in advance of his age; and there was no one left in Italy to continue his work of enlightenment when he died in 570.

Much more representative of the times were Benedict of Nursia and Gregory the Great, whose attitude to ancient learning is in strong contrast to that of Cassiodorus. Our knowledge of St. Benedict is derived mainly from the second book of the *Dialogues of St. Gregory the Great*, and from the text of the *Benedictine Rule*. It has been argued by those who wish to trace the enthusiasm for sacred learning characteristic of the Benedictine Order at a later period back to its founder, that St. Benedict established the study of the liberal arts in his monasteries at Monte Cassino and Subiaco. But if so, it is strange that we have no evidence of it either in the *Dialogues* or in the *Rule*. On the contrary, Gregory tells us in his preface to the second book of the *Dialogues* that Benedict, having seen the sad effects of learning upon his contemporaries, renounced it and retired into the desert knowingly ignorant and wisely foolish (*scienter nescius sapienter indoctus*). The 48th Chapter of the *Rule* ('Of Daily Manual Labour') ordains fixed hours for holy reading; but there is no evidence that this holy reading required any knowledge of the liberal arts, or anything more than the ability to read the sacred text and the Fathers. Had there been anything which deserves to be called scholarship at Monte Cassino in the days of St. Benedict, we should surely have had some theological work of importance from it. As it is, the only product of importance is the *Rule of St. Benedict*, which has no claim to beauty of style or correctness of language; so that we may conclude that the primitive Benedictines had not the love of learning which later on became inseparable from the order. This does not preclude the possibility of certain better educated men having joined the order in its early days—but the study of the humanities was in no sense part of the programme of its founder.

Gregory the Great (590–604) was a monk and pupil of St. Benedict, and his attitude to the liberal arts reflects that of his master. According to Gregory of Tours, Gregory the Great had studied grammar, rhetoric, and dialectic, but in later life he appears to have discontinued his early studies. He did not know Greek, and in a letter to his friend Leander of Seville he says that he avoids neither barbarisms nor solecisms—that is, he is content to use the ordinary ecclesiastical Latin of his day. On the same lines are his well-known words in the *Moralia*,[1] in which he expresses his contempt for the rules of grammarians, adding that he 'considers it positively disgraceful to fetter the language of the Holy Spirit with the rules of Donatus'. In his notorious letter to Desiderius of Vienne he tells him that he has heard with pain that Desiderius is teaching grammar to some, and that he is saddened to think that the same mouth should sing both of Jupiter and Christ, but he hopes that it is a false report that has reached him. Such statements show Gregory's contempt for literary form, mingled no doubt with fear of the dangers which the Faith might have to apprehend from too intimate an acquaintance with pagan authors.

The outlook for the future of the Fine Arts in Italy in the days of Gregory was not bright. It has been admirably described in a recent work.[2]

'The conversion of England begun by St. Augustine and his Roman Mission occurred at a time when Southern Europe and especially Italy was again in the melting-pot. The tide of Justinian's conquests had ebbed, the Lombards had overrun the country, a series of disasters, both natural and artificial, had overtaken the people, and to this was shortly to be added the arrival of a host of refugees from

---

[1] *P.* ix. lxxv. 516.

[2] A. W. Clapham's *English Romanesque Architecture before the Conquest* (1930).

Africa, Egypt, and Syria, displaced by the Moslem conquests. The results of these factors, the last excepted, on Italian art and architecture were deplorable; and Signor Cattaneo has shown how rapidly the art of sixth-century Italy disappeared in the seventh, and by what painful steps it gradually revived. It was from a rapidly decaying society that St. Augustine's Mission came.'

In this dark period of their history, the liberal arts found an asylum and haven of refuge in the British Isles, and it was the Anglo-Celtic Churches which restored them to the Continent.

The question naturally arises—how did the liberal arts reach the British Isles? It is a question easier to ask than to answer. Since Britain formed part of the Roman Empire, it is possible that the British Church inherited the study of the arts from the imperial schools, or they may have been a heritage from missionaries from Gaul. But this solution is inapplicable to Ireland, which never formed part of the Roman Empire. How then did the arts reach Ireland? There are three possible answers, none of which is susceptible of mathematical proof. We may hold with Zimmer that the study of the liberal arts was transmitted to Ireland by members of the British Church, or with Arbois de Jubainville that the Irish owed the arts to scholars who had fled to Ireland from Gaul to escape the barbarian invasions, or lastly (though I know of no evidence to support the view), we may assume that the study of the liberal arts was imported directly into Ireland by monks from Constantinople, Alexandria, or other Mediterranean places.

The history of classical learning in the ancient British Church need not detain us long, for it has little direct bearing upon the subject of our inquiry, though it may not have been without considerable influence upon Anglo-Saxon Latinity, particularly if Hisperic Latinity had its source in the schools of Wales. It may suffice to say that there is a continuous tradition of Latin learning in the British Church from the early part of the fourth century, though it is not until we reach the age of Gildas and the Anglo-Saxon invasions that we have irrefutable evidence of the existence of a knowledge of the liberal arts in Britain. Native tradition assigns to St. Cadoc the honour of having founded the schools of Wales, and credits him with a knowledge of Priscian, Donatus, and the arts, which he transmitted to his two most famous disciples Iltud and Gildas. The former was the founder of one of the most famous of the Welsh schools, the monastery of Llan-Iltud. Here, according to Zimmer, Iltud established a centre of rhetorical studies analogous to the schools of rhetoric in ancient Gaul. Zimmer traces to this school that wild scion of classical learning known as Hisperic Latin, and thinks that he can discern in the *Hisperica Famina* descriptions drawn from the school at Llan-Iltud. We are, however, on firmer ground when we ascribe to Gildas considerable knowledge of the arts. His famous work *De Excidio Britanniae*, despite its obscure and awkward style, is the work of a scholar. Mommsen has noted in it at least three reminiscences of Virgil and one of Juvenal, with echoes of Persius and Claudian. The traditions of the age of

Gildas were still carefully preserved in Wales when Augustine paid his famous visit to the British Church. Even Ethelfrith's victory at Chester, fatal to so many of the Welsh scholars, did not kill learning in Wales, for was it not from Wales that King Alfred got one of his most loyal helpers and his biographer Asser, whom he made bishop of Sherborne?

But the important part played by the Irish Church in the evangelization and dissemination of ancient culture both in England and on the Continent is an adequate reason for the greater importance attaching to the history of classical learning in Ireland.

The passionate enthusiasm with which the Irish devoted themselves to the study of sacred learning and the liberal arts from the seventh century is without parallel in the rest of Europe; its closest analogue is perhaps the welcome accorded to Roman rhetoric in the schools of Gaul in the fourth century.

It would seem unlikely that the earliest Christian missionaries to Ireland, whether from Britain or the Continent, had either leisure or inclination to give themselves up to the teaching of the arts. But in a very short time (as we have already seen) Ireland was covered with a network of monasteries, in which, by the seventh century, the study of sacred literature held the foremost place and was pursued with a thoroughness and intensity unknown elsewhere in Europe at that date. Latin was, of course, indispensable; nor did the study of the profane writers offer the same dangers to the Christians of Ireland as it did to the

Christians of Gaul, where the pagan religion of the Empire was still a serious rival of Christianity. Accordingly not only the holy scriptures (including many apocryphal writings) and the works of the Fathers, but also a wide range of profane authors were brought to Ireland, copied in the scriptoria of great Irish schools like Clonmacnoise, Bangor, Clonfert, or Moville, and studied with avidity by hundreds and even thousands of scholars who thronged the Irish schools from the sixth century onward.

Unfortunately, we have no description of the exact nature of the teaching given by the masters in these schools; but the writings of some of their alumni give us a clear notion of its range. Columbanus of Luxeuil was a pupil of St. Comgall, abbot of the famous monastic school of Bangor in northern Ireland—a school which remained celebrated until its destruction by the Danes in the first half of the ninth century. The writings of Columbanus show ability to write Latin fluently, if not always correctly, in both prose and verse. His writings on the paschal controversy reveal his training not only in the trivium but also in the quadrivium. As we should expect, he is intimately acquainted with the Bible and the works of the Latin Fathers, but, in addition, Columbanus frequently quotes or echoes Virgil, Ovid, Persius, Horace, and Sallust. His practice affords a striking contrast to that of his great contemporary St. Gregory. Nor does he stand alone: his practice is typical of that of his countrymen and successors. Cellanus of Peronne and Adamnan of Iona quote Virgil, while the elder Pliny, Cicero, Frontinus, Vegetius, Valerius Maximus, Macrobius, Donatus, Priscian, Boethius, and Martianus Capella are among classical writers quoted in Irish manuscripts before the close of the eighth century. Martianus Capella enjoyed a great vogue among the Irish both at home and abroad, and his influence upon Virgil of Salzburg, who, following him, maintained the existence of the antipodes against Boniface and the Pope, proves that the influence of the classics upon the Celts was not merely formal, but affected their thinking. The paschal controversy, which has been already referred to in connexion with St. Columbanus, forced the Irish to extend their knowledge of mathematics and astronomy. Krusch has shown that the work on the Paschal Cycle long ascribed to Anatolius of Laodicea was written in Ireland during the sixth century, and during the eighth and ninth centuries Celts like Dicuil and Dunchad were among the leading authorities on mathematics and astronomy. The intense love of learning and scholarship characteristic of the Irish has found delightful expression in an old Irish poem which was written by a student of the monastery of St. Paul, Carinthia, on a copy of the Epistles of St. Paul about the close of the eighth century. It has been most pleasingly translated by Mr. Robin Flower under the title of 'The Student and his Cat'.

> I and Pangur Ban, my cat,
> 'Tis a like task we are at;
> Hunting mice is his delight,
> Hunting words I sit all night.

Better far than praise of men
'Tis to sit with book and pen;
Pangur bears me no ill will,
He, too, plies his simple skill.

'Tis a merry thing to see
At our tasks how glad are we,
When at home we sit and find
Entertainment to our mind.

Oftentimes a mouse will stray
In the hero Pangur's way;
Oftentimes my keen thought set
Takes a meaning in its net.

'Gainst the wall he sets his eye
Full and fierce and sharp and sly;
'Gainst the wall of knowledge I
All my little wisdom try.

When a mouse darts from its den,
O! how glad is Pangur then;
O! what gladness do I prove
When I solve the doubts I love.

So in peace our task we ply,
Pangur Ban, my cat and I;
In our arts we find our bliss,
I have mine and he has his.

Practice every day has made
Pangur perfect in his trade;
I get wisdom day and night
Turning darkness into light.

In this connexion, a most important and yet rather difficult question is how much Greek was known by these Irish scholars. Eduard Norden[1] roundly says that the knowledge of Greek (*in the earlier Middle Ages*) which had almost died out in the West, was so widespread in Ireland, that it was assumed that if a man knew Greek he came from Ireland. There is also a widespread notion that a knowledge of Greek was typical of ancient Irish learning. I have not time to go into the evidence. I can only say here that it seems to be a question of dates. Recent scholarship inclines to the view that it is probable that the knowledge of Greek in Ireland before the close of the seventh century was such as could be got from glossaries, and that the introduction of Greek learning into the British Isles is to be ascribed to Theodore of Tarsus, Abbot Hadrian, and the school of Canterbury. But Norden's statement is true to this extent, that Theodore and Hadrian had no more eager pupils than the Irish (witness for example Aldhelm's complaints), and that the Irish were among the foremost exponents of Greek learning in the Carolingian era, when John Scotus Erigena won the admiration of his contemporaries by translating the *Celestial Hierarchy* of the Pseudo-Dionysius from Greek into Latin.

We may sum up this section of our inquiry by saying that while learning was almost extinct on the Continent it was vigorously alive in Ireland, whose schools attracted scholars from foreign lands. The Life of an Irish Saint (St. Senan) tells of seven vessels all full of

[1] Op. cit. 666.

students bound for the school of Inisceltra, dropping anchor at once off the mouth of the Shannon, and elsewhere (Angus the Culdee) we read of Britons, Romans, Latins, and seven Egyptian monks coming to Ireland in search of learning. We may be tempted to discount such stories and regard them as products of Irish imagination; but no such suspicion attaches to the Venerable Bede[1] who, speaking of the plague in Ireland in A.D. 664, says:

'This pestilence did no less harm in the island of Ireland. Many of the nobility, and of the lower ranks of the English, were there at that time, who, in the days of Bishops Finan and Colman, forsaking their native island retired thither, either for the sake of Divine Studies, or of a more continent life; and some of them presently devoted themselves to the monastic life, others chose rather to apply themselves to study, going about from one master's cell to another. The Irish willingly received them all, and took care to supply them with food, as also to furnish them with books to read and their teaching gratis.'

Among many others who visited the schools of Ireland at this period were Dagobert, king of the Franks, Aldfrith, king of Northumberland, Agilþert, the Frank, who afterwards became bishop of the West Saxons, championed Roman usage at the Conference of Whitby, and later became Bishop of Paris, St. Chad, bishop of Lichfield, St. Willibrord, the apostle of Friesland, and Egbert, the Northumbrian noble who persuaded

[1] *H.E.* iii. 27.

Iona to adopt the Catholic Easter, with his friend Ethelhun.

But, as we have already seen, the Irish themselves carried their learning far and wide. Learning went hand in hand with evangelization, and their monasteries were usually schools as well as missionary centres, from which men like Columba spread religion and learning among the Picts and Scots, Aidan in Northumbria, Columbanus and St. Gall in Switzerland, France, and Italy, St. Killian and Virgil of Salzburg in Thuringia and Carinthia.

In the eloquent words of A. W. Haddan:

'First by armies of missionaries, and then by learned teachers —first by attracting pupils to Irish schools from all Christian Europe North of the Alps and the Pyrenees, and next by sending men forth to become the founders of schools or monasteries or churches abroad, the Scottish (Irish) churches stand out from the sixth century forward as the most energetic centres of religious life and knowledge in Europe—the main restorers of Christianity in paganized England and Roman Germany—the reformers and main founders of monastic life in Northern France—the leading preservers, in the eighth and ninth centuries (though under strange guise), of theological culture, Greek as well as Latin—the scribes both at home and abroad of many a precious Biblical [and he might have added classical] text—the teachers of psalmody—the schoolmasters of the great monastic schools—the parents, in great part, as well as the forerunners, of Anglo-Saxon learning and missionary zeal.'[1]

[1] Haddan, *Remains*, 260.

Just as the English Church was, as we have tried to show, in some sense a blending of the Celtic and Roman systems with the native English temper, so Anglo-Saxon learning had a double source, Irish and Romano-Greek. In the lack of adequate knowledge of the range and extent of Irish schools in England before the age of Bede, it is difficult to estimate the debt of Anglo-Saxon learning to the Celtic Mission Church which played such an important part in their evangelization. We know that the Anglo-Saxon half-uncial hand was derived from the Irish hand, and that the Roman uncial never became popular in England. We know, too, that Irish schools were not confined to Northumbria, Mercia, and East Anglia, for was not Aldhelm, the most learned of the Anglo-Saxons, a pupil of the Irish scholar Maeldubh of Malmesbury, as well as of Theodore of Tarsus? Moreover, there is evidence in our Anglo-Saxon poetical texts that their authors drew upon sources of information which were banned by the Roman Church, though in favour with the Irish— I refer to the apocryphal writings condemned by a decree, erroneously ascribed to Pope Gelasius, 492–6, which fixed the canonical books of Scripture.

The influence of apocryphal writings upon Anglo-Saxon literature is an interesting subject which has not yet been adequately treated. It presents great difficulties, not the least of which is the unprinted condition of so many important works in ancient Irish. Its influence, of course, is obvious in works dealing with the Harrowing of Hell, but its presence is equally certain in Anglo-

Saxon Texts so well known as *Beowulf, Genesis A and B,* the *Andreas* and *Fates of the Apostles,* the *Exodus, Solomon and Saturn, Christ and Satan, Guthlac,* the *Blickling Homilies,* and other old English works in prose and verse. Among the apocryphal works quoted or referred to in Irish or Anglo-Saxon literature are the *Book of Enoch,* the *Apocalypse of Moses,* the Latin *Life of Adam and Eve, Jannes and Mambres,* the *History of Joseph and Asenath,* the *Gospel of Nicodemus,* and *The Acts of Pilate,* various apocryphal acts of Apostles, apocalypses of Peter, Paul, and Andrew, and the *Epistle of Christ to Abgarus.* The list could be extended, but sufficient has been said to show that the Anglo-Saxons extended their studies to realms of knowledge which are not represented in the catalogues of the great schools controlled by Roman orthodoxy.

It seems to be safe to say that the standard in sacred and secular learning among the Anglo-Saxons in the seventh century was set by the schools of Ireland, for the earliest Christian poetry—*Beowulf* and the so-called Caedmonian poems—presupposes a range of studies far beyond that encouraged by Gregory the Great and his school. Indeed we have no evidence that Augustine established a school at Canterbury at all except Bede's statement that Felix of Dunwich established a school there after the model of Kent, and the catalogues, whether authentic or not, of the books brought by Augustine represent a very limited range of study at Canterbury; whereas the school at Dunwich (about which we are almost equally ignorant) may have received the powerful aid of the learning and holiness of the Irish Saint Fursey, who began in East Anglia, two years after the coming of Felix, the apostolic labours which he concluded at Peronne in Gaul.

The history of Canterbury as a seat of learning begins with the arrival of Theodore of Tarsus and Benedict Biscop in 669: they were followed shortly afterwards by Abbot Hadrian. Theodore and Hadrian began a new era in Anglo-Saxon scholarship and the Roman mission was now placed for the first time, as regards learning, in a position of equality and even (in some ways) of superiority to the Irish mission church. Yet it should be noted that neither Theodore nor Hadrian belonged as scholars to the tradition of St. Gregory.

Theodore, a native of Tarsus, was born about 602 in Cilicia. He was, therefore, twenty years old when Mahomet began his mission, and thirty-five when Jerusalem was captured by the Infidels. His education, begun at Tarsus, was completed at Athens. By such training as Tarsus and Athens afforded, he became a sound Greek and Latin scholar, a philosopher, and a thorough adept in secular and divine literature. He was a man of sixty-five when he came to Rome, and his whole training had been Greek rather than Latin. He was a monk of the eastern tonsure, and his tonsure like that of St. Chad had to be completed in the Roman fashion. Such, very briefly, was the man who was selected in 668 by Pope Vitalian for the archbishopric of Canterbury and the task of reorganizing the Anglo-Saxon Church, when he had been barely two years at Rome and was already in his sixty-eighth year.

Hadrian, on the other hand, was an African by birth. An exile, like Theodore, he had been abbot of an Italian monastery. He had been offered the archbishopric of Canterbury but had refused it, suggesting his friend Theodore, whom he promised to accompany, as Vitalian seems to have had some doubts as to Theodore's orthodoxy. Hadrian was Theodore's equal, if not his superior in scholarship, and on his arrival in England he took over the abbacy of St. Peter's at Canterbury.

Benedict Biscop, who accompanied Theodore from Rome, was a thegn of Oswin of Northumbria. From 665 to 667 he had been a monk of Lerins, and held the abbacy of St. Peter's, Canterbury, for two years until Hadrian's arrival. An enthusiastic supporter of the Roman discipline and the reformed monasticism, he retired from Canterbury to his native Northumbria in 670, where with the support of Ecgfrith he set to work to introduce the rule of St. Benedict and built the great monastery of St. Peter's at Wearmouth in 674, followed five years later by a new foundation at Jarrow. Benedict repeatedly visited Rome and Gaul, and was not merely an indefatigable collector of books and relics, but a lover of fine art. In building his monasteries he employed French masons, and the architecture was modelled on the churches of Rome, the windows being filled with stained glass and lattice work, the work of foreign artists, who were no doubt glad to find in England a shelter from the storms which had driven them from their native lands.

THE TRANSMISSION OF ANCIENT CULTURE

What followed on the arrival of these three men, Theodore, Hadrian, and Benedict Biscop, may be described in the words of Bede,[1] who is referring especially to Theodore and Hadrian:

'And forasmuch as both of them were well read in sacred and secular literature, they gathered a crowd of disciples, and there daily flowed from them rivers of knowledge to water the hearts of their hearers; and, together with the books of holy writ, they also taught them the arts of ecclesiastical poetry, astronomy and arithmetic—A testimony of which is, that there are still living at this day some of their scholars, who are as well versed in the Greek and Latin tongues as in their own, in which they were born.'

Among the most famous Anglo-Saxon pupils of Theodore and Hadrian's school at Canterbury were Aldhelm, abbot of Malmesbury and Bishop of Sherborne, John of Beverley, bishop of Hexham, Oftfor of Worcester, Tobias of Rochester (a man of multifarious learning in Latin, Greek, and Anglo-Saxon), and Albinus, Hadrian's successor at Canterbury. These in their turn became teachers and spread the fame of the School of Canterbury all over England. Nor was the fame of Canterbury confined to England. Aldhelm tells us how Theodore was surrounded by a crowd of Irish scholars, whom he could scatter at his ease, 'rending them with the tusk of grammar, like a fierce boar hemmed in by growling hounds of the Molossian breed, or, like a valiant archer hard pressed by the close phalanx of the

[1] iv. 2.

enemy, piercing them through and through with the sharp arrows of chronography.'

This brief extract exemplifies a weakness in one who is famed as the most learned of Anglo-Saxon scholars, and who numbered kings and foreign scholars among his pupils and correspondents. Aldhelm of Malmesbury combined in his work the newer Roman and the older Celtic traditions, for he was at once a pupil of the Celtic School of Maeldubh and of the School of Canterbury. Tempting as it is to describe his work at greater length,[1] we can only say that in spite of much pretentiousness and bombast, his work displays an intimate acquaintance with and mastery of Latin literature—poetry, science, and theology—even if his knowledge of Greek has been greatly exaggerated. William of Malmesbury describes him as a man 'wonderful in each of his qualities and peerless in them all'. With his death in 709 the prestige of the south in scholarship passed to the two great schools of Northumbria, first to Jarrow, inseparably associated with the name of the Venerable Bede, and then to York.

The twin monastery of Wearmouth and Jarrow was the foundation of Benedict Biscop, who had endowed it with a great collection of artistic treasures and books collected in his repeated pilgrimages to Rome and Gaul. Before he died in 689 he had established a new type of monastery thoroughly disciplined by a model rule and 'pursuing knowledge as an end in itself', which to a large

---

[1] On Aldhelm and his library see M. R. James, *Two Ancient English Scholars* (Glasgow 1931).

extent replaced the older missionary settlements of the Celtic Church. Special care was devoted to the care and reproduction of books, and the Northumbrian monasteries began to rival the Irish in magnificent manuscripts like Ecgfrith's *Lindisfarne Gospels* and the famous *Codex Amiatinus* which Ceolfrid carried with him as a present to the Pope on his last journey to Rome in 716, when he died on the way. Ceolfrid, Wilfrid, Cuthbert, Acca, and John of Beverley are all names connected with the new monasticism in Northumbria. Of some of these we know much more than we know of Benedict Biscop and Ceolfrid, but it was in the main the work of these two to provide the basis of eighth-century learning. Without them there would hardly have been a Wearmouth and Jarrow with their splendid library, and without Wearmouth and Jarrow it is doubtful if we should have had Bede. As Bishop Stubbs has said, Wearmouth and Jarrow produced Bede, and through him the School of York, Alcuin, and the Carolingian school, on which the culture of the Middle Ages rested.

Bede entered Biscop's monastery of Wearmouth at the age of seven, and when he was eight years old he was transferred to the new foundation at Jarrow, where for fifty-four years he was to spend his life 'devoting', as he tells us, 'all my pains to the study of the scriptures; and amid the observance of monastic discipline and the daily charge of singing in the Church, it has ever been my delight to learn, or teach, or write.' Trained by teachers of both the Roman and Celtic tradition, he was in touch at Jarrow with Irish, Roman, and Gallican learning, and the Graeco-Roman learning of Theodore and Hadrian at Canterbury, and traces of each abound in the works which made his name famous all over Europe as a doctor of the Church.

The records which we possess of his quiet, unbroken life of devotion and scholarship allow us to picture the great teacher surrounded by his pupils, as he initiated them into the various branches of learning of which he was himself a master. With Bede all learning was subsidiary to theology. His first task would be to teach his pupils the rudiments of the sacred tongue, to correct their barbarisms and solecisms, to expound the rules of accent and orthography so far as he understood them, and to proceed thence to the translation and exposition of the sacred text with the aid of Greek and even of Hebrew. His method is clear from his extant commentaries. Having explained the literal meaning of the text, he proceeds to unfold the mystical or allegorical significance which for him and his age lay behind the letter of the text. In doing so he employs all the profane and sacred learning at his disposal—knowledge of the tropes and figures of rhetoric, the commentaries of the Fathers, the recognized authorities upon sacred and secular history, and the natural sciences. The chanting of the Psalms, Hymns, and antiphones used in the daily services of the Church required a knowledge of Latin accentuation and even of prosody; while the necessity of making no mistakes about the correct date of Easter and the movable feasts of the Church led to an intensive study of the computus, chronology, and astronomy. Bede's patriotism, as well as his keen interest in the ecclesiastical and political controversies and conditions of his own age, made him the first historian of medieval Europe and its master in chronology. In spite of some defects, his *Ecclesiastical History* shows a critical power astounding for its age, while its method and style, and above all the personality which shines through the style, have made it one of the classics of human history. The Venerable Bede died in the year 735, and with him the fame of Jarrow as the foremost centre of learning in Anglo-Saxon England. The position held by Jarrow now passed to York, where a new centre of learning had been founded which owed its European fame to three famous scholars, Egbert, archbishop of York, 732–66, Albert, or Ethelbert, and above all Alcuin.

The origins of the School of York are obscure: it is probable that it was in existence before Egbert's day, but its fame as a centre of the study of the liberal arts dates from Egbert's accession. Egbert was brother of Eadbert, king of the Northumbrians. Tradition makes him a pupil of Bede; at all events he was his close friend, and on his accession Bede wrote to him the famous letter describing the decadent condition of the Church in Northumbria, in which he tells the new archbishop that the Church is full of disorder, corruption, and luxury, and in need of the most vigorous and searching reform. Bede's advice did not fall on deaf ears, and Egbert proved a most learned and capable prelate. But we are here concerned only with his services to learning. His own literary works, which are mainly of a practical nature, having for their aim the elevation and disciplining of the Church, were held in great repute, but his chief title to fame is the care which he took of the School of York attached to the Minster. Egbert was himself the head of the School and taught theology, while Abbot Albert taught grammar, rhetoric, law, poetry, astronomy, natural history, arithmetic, geometry, computation of the date of Easter, and Sacred Scripture. Alcuin gives us a pleasing glimpse of Egbert as a teacher. Among other things he tells us that when dinner was over 'it was a pleasure to him to hear his scholars discuss literary questions. In the evening he said compline with them, and then each received his blessing, kneeling at Egbert's feet.' Scholars flocked to York from all over Europe. It is a curious fact that when Northumbria politically was falling into a hopeless state of decay, 'the discipline and learning of Egbert were enlightening other countries than that which they were intended to humanize'. Egbert's most famous pupil was Alcuin, but Alcuin's most lasting work was done in Germany and France, not in his native land.

Alcuin was born *c.* 735, the year in which Bede died. He belonged to the noble Northumbrian house from which Saint Willibrord of Friesland sprang. In his early childhood he was sent to the school at York, where he was a favourite pupil of Albert and Egbert. He was a promising pupil, and Egbert prophesied great things for his future. His proficiency in study awakened the jealousy of his fellow students, but Alcuin won their friendship and admiration by his modesty and goodness. He became the close friend of Albert, and accompanied him on several journeys to the Continent to collect books for the famous library which was one of the glories of the School of York, in which Alcuin himself was now appointed a teacher. In 766 Egbert died and Abbot Albert became archbishop, while Alcuin succeeded Albert as teacher of grammar, the arts, and sciences. The range of Alcuin's learning, and the contribution which the School of York, through him, was capable of making to the Continent can be best gauged from the catalogue of books in the library. It is given by Alcuin in his 'Poem on the Church of York'. It includes in the first place the Fathers of the Church—Jerome, Hilary, Ambrose, Augustine, Athanasius, St. Gregory, Leo, St. Basil, Fulgentius, Chrysostomos; Christian writers like Orosius, Lactantius, Sedulius, Juvencus, Avitus, Prudentius, Prosper, Paulinus, Arator, and Fortunatus; classical authors including Trogus, Pompeius, Pliny, Aristotle, Cicero, Virgil, Statius, Lucan, with Cassiodorus and Boethius; and a long list of grammarians, Victorinus, Probus, Donatus, Priscian, Servius, Eutyches, Cominianus, and Phocas. The list is probably not complete—St. Isidore was almost certainly represented at York. What strikes one most is the orthodox character of the writers named. No apocryphal work occurs, nor any writer whose opinions rendered him suspect. To provide such works was the privilege of the Irish, whose fondness for so dangerous a text as Martianus Capella was notorious.

Had Alcuin remained in England, he would no doubt have been remembered as one of the most famous among Anglo-Saxon scholars; but his fame would have remained overshadowed by the greater name of the Venerable Bede. But it was Alcuin's fortune, when a man of some sixty years, to be called to a land where his learning and his ability as a teacher placed him *facile princeps*.

As we have seen, learning had become almost extinct in the Frankish Empire under the Merovingians. The Church reforms inaugurated by St. Boniface, with the co-operation of Carloman and Pippin, demanded a higher standard of knowledge in the clergy, and already there were signs of a renaissance in centres such as Utrecht, Fulda, Metz, St. Gall, and Salzburg, as well as here and there throughout France.

The accession of Charles the Great brought to the throne a man of whom it has been said that he showed as much joy in winning a scholar for his service as in capturing a city. Anyhow, Charles was determined to make his kingdom first in letters as well as in military and political power among the kingdoms of Europe. He loved learning, though he had not the education which enabled his greatest rival in fame, Alfred the Great, to write books himself. But Charles had the gift of choosing men, and his choice was not limited by national prejudices. From Ireland, England, Spain, and Italy he summoned scholars to his aid. His love

THE TRANSMISSION OF ANCIENT CULTURE 107

of foreigners, particularly of the Irish, was made a reproach to him. Under Charles the palace school at Aix became a kind of university. Hither came Peter of Tuscany, a master of grammar and irony. More famous still was Paulus Diaconus, the historian of the Lombards who spent four years (782–6) with Charles, and with Peter of Tuscany brought to Charles some of the fruit of the reviving classical studies of eighth-century Italy. From Spain came Saint Theodulph of Orleans, to whom we owe the familiar hymn 'All glory, laud and honour'. Clement and Dunchad came from Ireland, while other notable helpers were Paulinus of Aquileia, the Bavarian Arno, and Leidrad.

Gifted as each of these men was in various ways, none of them was entirely suited for Charles's purpose, nor completely won his confidence. Charles found the man he wanted in Alcuin, whom he met probably not for the first time at Parma in 781.

'In Alcuin were united all the qualifications which Charles desired. A man of Teutonic race; learned with a learning far above the level of the age; a born teacher; pupil and master of York, which was then the greatest school in Europe; sober, methodical, orthodox, and conservative; imbued, above all, with the profoundest respect and admiration for Charles himself, and the completest sympathy with his ecclesiastical aspirations; he was the ideal scholar for Charles's purpose.'

To sketch the course of the Carolingian Renaissance is beyond my present scope. All that can be said here is that the palace school under Alcuin's superintendence became the centre of a revival of interest in literature and art which permeated the Frankish Empire. The educational system of the Empire was reorganized; the education of the Clergy was reformed; the liturgy was revised; the text of the Vulgate, which had suffered much from the ignorance of scribes, was corrected; and in the *scriptoria* at Tours and Orleans a new script was evolved, which became the famous Carolingian hand.

The Anglo-Saxon tradition was passed by Alcuin to Hrabanus Maurus of Fulda, and from Hrabanus to Wallafrid Strabo and Heric of Auxerre, who, in his turn, was one of the most famous teachers of the early schools at Rheims and Paris. Odo of Cluny, a pupil of Remy, was the protagonist in the classical revival, to which tenth-century England owes so much. Eighth-century England, through Boniface and Alcuin (with many less famous Anglo-Saxons), transmitted the sacred and profane learning which she herself had received from the Celtic Church and the Graeco-Roman schools represented by Theodore, Hadrian, and Benedict Biscop. Walter Pater, in a different connexion, says, 'The devotion of the father then had handed on loyally —and that is all many not unimportant persons ever find to do—a certain tradition of life.' Anglo-Saxon England has no claim to compete with the Athens of Pericles or the Rome of Augustus; but the devotion of the Anglo-Saxons of the seventh and eighth centuries saved much of the classical and sacred learning handed down to them from the Graeco-Roman world by transmitting it to the Frankish Empire a generation before the cataclysm of the Danish Invasion burst upon the schools of England, as it burst on those of Ireland, where for some three centuries learning banished from the rest of Europe had found a welcome and a home.